TRAVELLING NEW ZEALAND
A GUIDE TO 45 TOP VISITOR DESTINATIONS

Text by Simon Henshaw

Maps by Roger Smith, Geographx

craig potton publishing

To my parents, Richard and Jennifer,
who expanded my horizons beyond the concrete cityscape and into the natural world.

First published in 2007 by Craig Potton Publishing

Craig Potton Publishing
98 Vickerman Street, PO Box 555, Nelson, New Zealand
www.craigpotton.co.nz

© Text: Craig Potton Publishing
© Maps: Geographx

ISBN 13: 978-1-877333-66-8

Printed in China by Midas Printing International Ltd

CONTENTS

INTRODUCTION

With its natural beauty and modern, outdoor lifestyle, New Zealand is indeed a lucky country, most renowned for its beautiful landscapes and friendly people. That our natural landscapes are crammed into a few small islands within the same land area as Colorado makes them all that much closer and accessible. We have also achieved a unique and relatively harmonious mix of cultures and ethnicities, and have an enviable reputation for our friendliness, and for offering a warm welcome.

I have been privileged enough to travel this country my entire life, first with my parents, brother and sister on family holidays and then while guiding friends and clients throughout the country during the past 10 years. Even my honeymoon was spent tramping on Stewart Island and sailing the Abel Tasman coastline.

The diverse and dramatic scenery, from the majestic Southern Alps, to the ruggedly diverse coastlines surrounding the entire country inspires me to share this special place with overseas visitors, and to encourage New Zealanders to travel and appreciate their own country. I continually explore areas and activities off the beaten track and away from mass tourism, and where possible, have included as many lesser-known options as possible.

Scope and Purpose of this Book

Travelling New Zealand does not present a comprehensive list of everything to do in all parts of New Zealand. Instead, it aims to help you cut through the information avalanche that invariably strikes when planning a holiday. With websites, blogs, travel guides and information centres, the sheer quantity of information on areas and activities can be overwhelming. This book aims to give you the best things to do in the top New Zealand areas so you can spend more time enjoying yourself and less time interpreting the marketing hype of various brochures. It cuts through the countless options available for filling your time, enabling you to select locations, activities and tours that provide an authentic experience and insight into the nature, history and culture of that place.

Maps by Geographx

Geographx is a digital mapping company that uses digital imaging and K2Vi virtual reality mapping technology to create incredible, almost-3D representations of New Zealand landscapes from any angle. This cutting-edge technology enables a nearly photographic-quality presentation of landscape features including vegetation, natural shading and snow-cover. The resulting aerial panoramas enhance the viewer's perception of the landform and communicate the location's qualities more effectively than regular topographic maps. Visit www.geographx.co.nz for more information.

Featured Attractions and Activities

The attractions and activities featured in this book are a mix of the 'must see' New Zealand icons, the 'most popular' as recommended by regional tourism organisations, and a whole lot of really interesting, but lesser-known little places, cafes, activities and walking tracks which I personally know and am delighted to share with you.

Each region commonly produces its own brochures focusing on subjects such as arts and crafts, historical places, etc so I have not included all of these – pick them up when you arrive. In many locations there are local tour operators that can give you a guided introduction to attractions, local history, and local walking tracks. Some options have been included but not an exhaustive list. Where there are several operators providing a similar experience we have focused our information on the experience rather than one operator as service standards and safety are pretty high on most occasions.

Missing but not Forgotten

The maps in this book are as much a feature as the writing. Because of this, some of my favourite places or attractions have been left out, as they lie between the featured destinations. This includes places such as the Moeraki Boulders, the Oamaru historic precinct, Whanganui National Park, New Plymouth, Tauranga, Cape Palliser and especially Kapiti Island. Typically, the numbers of people visiting these areas are not huge enough to warrant inclusion, but their very seclusion makes them all the more attractive. If the concept of this book proves successful, we may be able to include them in the next edition.

Seasonality

New Zealand's busy touring season is overwhelmingly between November and March. Outside of these months some businesses will reduce their hours or options, or even close altogether. Call ahead to check the open hours and options available.

Booking Ahead

Many of the commercial activities mentioned in this book are very popular and/or have restrictions on frequency or participant numbers due to conservation values or operational capacity. We recommend you book activities and accommodation well ahead if possible. During the busiest period from mid-December right through February, booking at least three months ahead will ensure you aren't disappointed. If that hasn't been possible, do call ahead as much as practicable. Some operators offer concessions on 'early bird' or off-peak departures. This has the advantage of getting you out of bed a little earlier, saving some money, and more often than not, enjoying the experience without the same volume of people. During the quieter periods, phoning ahead will ensure you don't turn up to a 'Closed' sign.

A general rule of thumb: Do your research well in advance and if you know you would be disappointed if you miss out on a particular service, book it now.

Conservation & Safety

As you travel around New Zealand please take steps to minimise your impacts on the environment: select activities and accommodation that demonstrate sustainable business practices; remove your rubbish; consider noise and its effects on others. Regarding safety, New Zealand is a pretty safe place but the usual precautions should be taken: mind your valuables; be aware of your personal safety; and keep your vehicle seating area as clear as possible. Put as much as possible out of sight in the boot: jackets, travel books, sunglasses…

Walking Tracks

Walking and tramping (hiking) experiences are described in brief. For detailed information about track conditions and features, and a complete list of these opportunities please visit the local i-Site visitor information centre or Department of Conservation office (DOC). Ensure that a track is suitable for your fitness level before getting started. New Zealand weather can change quickly so always check the forecast and take appropriate wet-weather clothing, food and drink, and always tell someone where you're going, when you expect to be back, or leave your name in the DOC intentions book at the beginning of some tracks.

Accuracy of Information

The attractions and locations have been chosen subjectively based on my own experience and the recommendations of regional tourism organisations and information centres. Every effort has been made to ensure that the information in this book is as accurate and up-to-date as possible; however, errors may still exist. If you find significant errors please write to the publishers so that future editions may be improved.

Best wishes for a wonderful holiday
SIMON HENSHAW

THE FAR NORTH

The Far North of New Zealand is believed to have been the location for the first arrival of voyagers from Polynesia roughly 1000 years ago. Today the Maori and Pakeha residents of the Far North enjoy a subtropical lifestyle whose climate is dictated by the surrounding oceans. The land north of Kaitaia could be described as an enormous sand dune built up by the Tasman Sea and Pacific Ocean. With sandy beaches facing west, north and east there is always an opportunity for surfing or surf fishing.

Despite being slightly off the beaten path of mainstream tourism this region has many wonderful, easily reached natural places and well-organised visitor services. Base yourself in the Bay of Islands, or stay at one of the many small lodges or Bed and Breakfasts that are well located with coastal or farmland views.

❶ Puketi and Omahuta Forest Walks
These forests are rich with native vegetation, birdlife and opportunities to escape the sounds of humanity. A number of short and long tracks explore the impressive stands of kauri that have survived the early logging industry. Some short tracks are boardwalked for easy access. Further information on individual tracks can be found at DOC visitor centres.

❷ Kaitaia
A service town for the surrounding farming community, from where many tour operators start their Cape Reinga trips. Seven km north of the town is the Ancient Kauri Kingdom and café where you will find exquisite furniture and crafts carved from ancient swamp kauri.

❸ Ninety Mile Beach
Perhaps New Zealand's most famous beach (actually only 88 km or 55 miles), great for a paddle, surf casting, and searching for shellfish. Brave souls like to risk their vehicles by driving along this sandy 'alternative road'. Check your rental car agreement though as most companies will prohibit this, and beware the quicksand, sand holes and slippery plankton build-ups! There are several places to reach the beach.

❹ Cape Reinga and Spirits Bay
The Pacific Ocean mixes with the Tasman Sea under the watchful eye of a 1941 lighthouse and lone pohutukawa tree at the most north-western tip of the North Island. According to Maori legend the spirits of the recently deceased travel via Cape Reinga to the afterlife in the spiritual homeland of Hawaiki. There are spectacular views, and several walking tracks for exploring the Cape and Spirits Bay.

❺ Te Paki Sand Dunes
At 100 metres high and travelling inland for 5 km, these giant sand dunes, made of soft silica sand, are formed by the predominant westerly wind from the Tasman Sea. Hire a toboggan from Ahipara and enjoy some exhilarating fun, or climb to the top of a dune for some quiet contemplation within this dramatic landscape.

❻ The Hokianga Harbour
Small villages are scattered around this natural harbour, each with a story to tell of early Maori and European settlement. The Copthorne Hotel at Omapere is our pick of the places to stay, with views of the harbour entrance and massive sand dunes opposite. Enjoy a quiet coffee or a glass of wine in its traditional public bar before this character-filled slice of kiwiana is renovated, or outside on the lovely, sweeping verandah. A car ferry crosses between Rawene and Rangiora.

❼ Matakohe Kauri Museum
A visit to this museum will provide an interesting and in-depth understanding of the Kauri tree, the world's second largest tree, and how its exquisite timber has been exported around the world for furniture, ship-building, carving and more. Extensive displays include milling equipment, kauri furniture, kauri gum and the pioneer history of the area.

❽ Waipoua Kauri Forest
Public pressure during the 1940s and early 1950s finally saved this magnificent native forest from the destructive practices of early European settlers. Kauri timber and gum was highly prized, and vast tracts of land were cleared for farmland. Waipoua Forest is today the largest remaining area of native forest in the Northland region and home to Tane Mahuta, New Zealand's largest living kauri tree. Explore the multitude of tracks (some boardwalked) to observe the diverse variety of trees, plants and birdlife. Several parking areas have volunteers preventing car break-ins, for which a few dollars is obligatory.

Pacific Ocean

N

...ikari Peninsula

...ubtless Bay

Mangonui

Whangaroa Harbour

Whangaroa

Matauri Bay

Cavalli Islands

Takou Bay

Bay of Islands

Cape Brett

Kerikeri

1

Omahuta / Puketi Forests

Russell

Paihia

Whangaruru Harbour

Kaikohe

Kawakawa

Poor Knights Is.

Waipoua Kauri Forest

Tutukaka

WHANGAREI

Dargaville

Bream Bay

Wairoa River

Matakohe Kauri Museum

7

Brynderwyn

Ruawai

Kaipara Harbour

BAY OF ISLANDS

The Bay of Islands lives up to its name, with 144 islands of various sizes. The name was bestowed by Captain James Cook who explored the area in November 1769. After he departed Europeans began visiting and settling in ever increasing numbers and today, after a tumultuous history of Maori and British interaction, it has become a favourite playground for holiday-makers and yachties from all points of the compass. The secluded bays and sandy beaches of the mainland and many islands are open for public enjoyment with warm water, lush vegetation and coastal views. Marine life is abundant – dolphins can regularly be seen, and on less frequent occasions, whales and penguins.

Spread around the Bay are the main centres of Paihia, Waitangi, Russell and Kerikeri, each one suitable as a base for exploring the Far North, and each one providing a selection of historic attractions, nature experiences, culinary delights, fishing trips and other visitor services.

❶ Kawakawa

Kawakawa is a small town located at the junction of the main roads between Whangarei, the Bay of Islands and Kaitaia. Stop here for cafés, supplies and the main attraction – the public toilets created by Austrian-born artist Frederick Hundertwasser in 1998. These functioning toilets are a work of art combining ceramic, glass, copper, cobblestone, a living tree and even a grass roof.

❷ Paihia

Often regarded as the most popular vacation centre in the area, in Paihia you will find cruise, scuba diving, deep-sea fishing, sailing and a multitude of other activity and transport operators. An excellent selection of cafés and restaurants utilise fresh, locally-caught seafood. There's a couple of easily accessed local walks, one to view the bay at Paihia View Point (1 hour return), and another (1 hour return) through the Harrison's Bush Scenic Reserve. For those that like things less active, catch up on some local history in the public library – one of the friendliest and most charming in the country.

❸ Waitangi

In 1833 James Busby arrived and settled here, tasked by the British government with bringing some semblance of law and order to 'the hellhole of the Pacific'.

Bay of Islands

Piercy Is. (Hole in the Rock)
Cape Brett

Okahu Is.

Motukiekie Is.

Urupukapuka Is.

Cape Brett Peninsula

Moturua Is.

7

Motuarohia Is.

4 Russell

Russell Peninsula

Manawaora Bay

Okiato

5 Opua

Waikare Inlet

Karetu River

RUSSELL FOREST

N

Despite a lack of resources, Busby achieved some historic successes including the Declaration of Independence in 1835 and the signing of the Treaty of Waitangi in 1840. The Treaty House, the nearby gardens, the 35-metre-long Maori waka (canoe) and the national marae (meeting house) known as Te Whare Runanga are all open to visit. Guided tours are available and impart a greater understanding of New Zealand history.

4 Russell

Russell was the first place in New Zealand to be permanently settled by Europeans (in the 1830s), and so has a wealth of history. Its early reputation was less than pristine however with visiting sailors causing no end of mayhem. The main historical attractions include Flagstaff Hill, Pompallier House, Russell Museum and the bullet-holed Christ's Church (New Zealand's oldest church). Some lovely accommodation is available, complemented by excellent restaurants. Russell is located on the mainland but by far the easiest way to get there is by passenger-ferry from Paihia or car-ferry from Opua.

5 Opua

From Opua you can catch a car-ferry across to Okiato, before driving to Russell. Along the Okiato-Russell road you will find several wineries and scenic reserves.

6 Kerikeri

Kerikeri is a popular summer town with many historic sites from early European settlement. These include New Zealand's oldest stone building, the Stone Store (1832) and the Mission House, New Zealand's oldest wooden house (1821). Local artisans abound, including potters and painters. When in season you must try the local kiwifruit and oranges that thrive in this warm, sun-drenched region.

7 Cruising the Bay of Islands

If you left your yacht at home there is a variety of local sailing, cruising and fishing options available. Most operators collect their passengers from Paihia. Try the 'Cream Trip' cruise, visit the Hole in the Rock, or perhaps take a day-sail on the tall ship *R. Tucker Thompson*. You can even learn to sail or cast a line for marlin, tuna or snapper.

AUCKLAND CITY

Otara Markets 10

SH1 to HAMILTON

One Tree Hill, 8
Cornwall Park

Manukau Road

Mt Eden
1

Kelly Tarltons Underwater World

9

Newmarket 4

Parnell Village 4

5 Museum

Auckland
Domain

ferry to Hauraki Gulf Islands

4
Devonport Village

Art Gallery 7

Aotea Square

10

Queen Street

Ponsonby Rd

4

2 Sky Tower

Ferries ■

Stanley Bay

6 Maritime Museum

Viaduct Basin ■

Westhaven
Marina

Bayswater

3

Harbour Bridge

Waitemata Harbour

N

Birkenhead

SH1 to
WHANGAREI, NORTHLAND

Zoo

Auckland is New Zealand's largest metropolitan area, the city of sails and, more significantly, the largest Polynesian city in the world. With 1.3 million people of all races living in the four cities that make up Greater Auckland, this is a busy, vibrant cosmopolitan region.

Auckland is located at the narrowest point of mainland New Zealand. With two large harbours, 48 extinct volcanic cones, hundreds of kilometres of coastline and dozens of offshore islands, this city has plenty of opportunity for outdoor adventure. The climate is warm, averaging between 19–24°C in the summertime, and with a low rainfall that occurs frequently but not heavily.

1 Mt Eden
Of Auckland's 48 volcanic cones Mt Eden is the highest at 196 m, with great views from the top. Follow Mt Eden Road, then take a sharp left turn into the Mt Eden Domain (watch out for cattle).

2 Sky Tower
Rising 328 m above the city, the Sky Tower is easily found. At the top, three observation decks offer 360-degree views of Auckland. And if you can't face the cramped interior of the elevator again, take the fast way down by jumping off with Sky Jump (with wires attached). Open from 8.30 am every day.

3 Auckland Harbour Bridge Climb
There are several high places around Auckland for great city views, but the satisfaction and enjoyment must be greater when you climb your way to the top. So climb the Auckland Harbour Bridge! Guided tours, with commentary and all the safety gear you could wish for, take 1.5 hours. Trips depart from the Westhaven Marina, on the south side of the bridge.

4 Shop 'Til You Drop
Parnell Village has art galleries, crafts and souvenirs, fashion and jewellery, salons and cafés occupying the heritage buildings of Auckland's oldest suburb. Newmarket has fashion galore, beauty , gift shops, restaurants and entertainment. Ponsonby Road has a feast of cafés, bars, food shops, fashion and gifts. The historic Devonport Village across the harbour from downtown Auckland has charmingly renovated Victorian villas, relaxing cafés and many art galleries presenting ceramics, paintings and sculptures.

5 Auckland Museum
Auckland Museum sits atop a hill in the Auckland Domain, overlooking the city and harbour. Within the Greek-style colonnades of this heritage building you will find natural, cultural and social history from New Zealand and the Pacific, combined with a memorial to honour New Zealand's war dead. Open daily between 10 am and 5 pm. A donation of $5 is appreciated.

6 Maritime Museum and Viaduct Basin Yacht Harbour
The waterfront area between the orange-coloured Ferry Building and Viaduct Basin is a pleasant and interesting stroll. Along the way you will pass the DOC office, Fuller's ferry services, Maritime Museum, the marina that hosted the 2003 America's Cup and a host of cafés and restaurants.

7 Auckland Art Gallery
Auckland Art Gallery has the country's largest public collection of New Zealand and international art. A special feature is work by Maori and Pacific Island artists from the mid-1900s to the present day, integrating different aspects of their cultures through a variety of contemporary and modern media. It is located on the corner of Wellesley and Kitchener streets, 3 minutes walk from downtown Queen Street. Open daily between 10 am–5 pm, with free entry to the main galleries.

8 One Tree Hill, Cornwall Park
This 182-metre-high volcanic cone still clearly shows the remnants of early Maori fortifications. It was named for a single tree that once stood there. Successive trees have come and gone, with some controversy, but today only an obelisk graces the summit in honour of the Maori people. Also located in Cornwall Park is the Stardome Observatory and multi-media Planetarium.

9 Kelly Tarlton's Antarctic Encounter and Underwater World
Kelly Tarlton's is an interactive underground aquarium and Antarctic habitat located on Tamaki Drive, 10 minutes east of downtown Auckland. Stingrays, sharks, penguins, piranha and seahorses are just a few of the many marine species encountered. Open daily between 9 am and 6 pm (last admission at 5 pm).

10 Weekend Markets
Otara's Saturday market offers a spicy mix of Asian, Indian, Pacific and European food, fresh fruit, vegetables and Pacific Island arts and crafts. Aotea Square on Queen Street hosts a popular market on Fridays and Saturdays between 10 am and 6 pm, with traditional Maori and Pacific arts and crafts, organic and ethnic food, and fashion by innovative local designers.

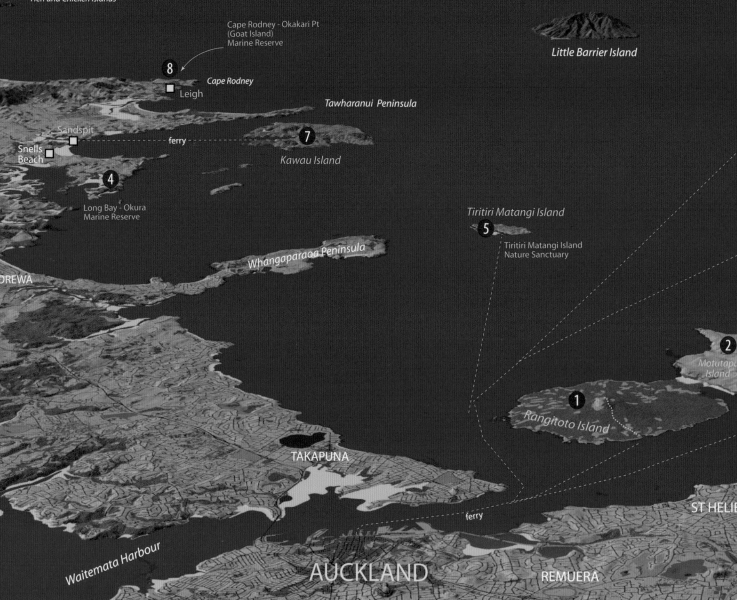

Hen and Chicken Islands

Mokohinau Islands

Cape Rodney - Okakari Pt
(Goat Island)
Marine Reserve

8

Cape Rodney

Leigh

Little Barrier Island

Tawharanui Peninsula

Sandspit — — — ferry — — —

Snells
Beach

7

Kawau Island

4

Long Bay - Okura
Marine Reserve

Tiritiri Matangi Island

5

Tiritiri Matangi Island
Nature Sanctuary

Whangaparaoa Peninsula

OREWA

2

*Motutapu
Island*

1

Rangitoto Island

TAKAPUNA

ST HELIER

ferry

Waitemata Harbour

AUCKLAND

REMUERA

Auckland's greatest natural assets are offshore in the Hauraki Gulf. For the 1.3 million citizens of Auckland, the Gulf is a different world; a complete contrast to city life only a few minutes away. While yachts and boats of every description are essential equipment for the locals, visitors can access this watery playground with the assistance of scheduled sailing excursions and ferry trips. Several fixed-wing and helicopter operators also provide access to the islands.

Select from the half-dozen islands discussed below according to how you like your island-time: completely wild and natural, remote with a pinch of civilisation, or bursting with cafés and vineyards. Also worth visiting are several marine reserves on the eastern coast of the mainland.

❶ Rangitoto Island

There's no mistaking Rangitoto. Its distinctive volcanic cone can be easily spotted from downtown Auckland and you can get there via Fuller's Ferries. Although now extinct, Rangitoto is relatively young, joining Auckland's volcanic party in spectacular fashion around 600 years ago. Walking tracks begin gently as they lead up to the summit, passing through a basalt lava-strewn landscape, slowly but surely being colonised by beautiful pohutukawa trees. Enjoy the 360-degree views, explore a lava cave, and have a picnic lunch. Another way to reach the top is by 4WD road-train.

❷ Motutapu Island

Motutapu Island was inhabited by Maori when Rangitoto burst into life 600 years ago. Roads and tracks lead across the island, most of which is farmland, but with many wetlands and patches of native vegetation being restored. The long Maori history here is evident with widespread sites of archaeological significance. Motutapu is accessible by regular, scheduled ferry services.

❸ Waiheke Island

Located only 35 minutes away by ferry, Waiheke is the Gulf's most populous island and home for many people who commute to Auckland city on a daily basis for work. For visitors the vineyards, art galleries, beaches and restaurants make for great fun and entertainment during a day or multi-day visit. Guided tours take in these attractions and more. A car ferry is available for transporting your car, but cars and scooters can be hired on the island and are the most efficient and convenient way to get around. Those seeking exercise can hire a bike but be prepared for a few hill climbs. Buses and taxis are the other transport options.

❹ Long Bay – Okura Marine Reserve

This marine reserve is approximately 30 minutes drive north of Auckland and protects sandy beaches, reefs and estuarine habitats. Since the reserve was

established in 1997 the fish and shellfish have recovered so well that the adjacent ocean areas (which are open to fishing and harvesting) are also more abundant. This is a popular place for swimming, snorkelling, picnics and exploring the rock pools.

5 Tiritiri Matangi Island Nature Sanctuary

The slightly longer ferry journey to Tiritiri Matangi Island is well rewarded by a feast of native birdlife and regenerating forest. The Department of Conservation removed all pest species before re-introducing rare and threatened species including kiwi, takahe, saddleback, parakeet and whitehead. Visitors can explore on their own, but joining a tour by volunteer guides is highly recommended. Overnight stays in basic accommodation are very popular and must be booked well ahead.

6 Great Barrier Island/Aotea

Sparsely populated, Great Barrier Island/Aotea has a mixture of farmland, rugged bush-covered hills and sandy beaches. This is a great location for getting away from it all in true Kiwi style. Hike along endless tracks, take a dip in natural hot springs, or explore historic sites left behind from the days of kauri forestry. Other activities include golf, fishing and sea kayaking. Accommodation can be found in quiet, secluded locations — try a 'bach' for basic needs, or luxury options for the finer touches. Driving around the island is perhaps the easiest and most convenient way to explore it. You can take your car there by scheduled SeaLink ferry (4 hours). Great Barrier Airlines fly there from Auckland several times each day.

7 Kawau Island

Kawau Island is an hour north of Auckland city and presents an unusual mix of colonial New Zealand history and introduced wildlife. Sir George Grey, the first Governor of New Zealand, built the stately Mansion House here and brought over a large number of exotic animals and trees. Peacocks and wallabies may be observed as you explore the Mansion House, forest, old Maori pa sites and beaches via a network of walking tracks. Kawau can be reached by scheduled ferry from Sandspit, located to the west of Kawau on the mainland.

8 Goat Island – Leigh Marine Reserve

Just over a 1 hour drive north of Auckland is the Goat Island Marine Reserve — New Zealand's first marine reserve. It's very popular with families as the fish are plentiful and friendly, and is great for swimming, snorkelling and scuba-diving. A glass-bottomed boat cruises the reserve allowing people to observe underwater life without getting wet. Our recommendation: get a snorkel and goggles and get wet!

Muriwai Beach

3 **4** Muriwai Gannet Colony

6 Goldie Bush walkway

Te Henga walkway

Lake Wainamu

WAITAKERE

5 **1**

Te Henga (Bethells Beach)

Piha **7**

8

Karekare Beach

N

If the Hauraki Gulf is the playground for Auckland's water-babies, the conveniently close Waitakere Ranges are where the land-lubbers go.

1 Waitakere Ranges Regional Park

Although not huge in a vertical sense (maximum 474 m above sea level) the Waitakere Ranges Regional Park covers around 160 sq km of land. The subtropical native forest within the park is recovering from earlier forestry incursions. Criss-crossing the park are hiking and mountain-biking tracks of varying difficulty.

Along the coast you will find several popular beaches with black sand. Be careful when swimming at these beaches as dangerously strong rips and swift currents make this a risky activity. Only swim where and when lifeguards are on duty and follow their directions. Popular beaches include Piha, Cornwallis, Karekare and Te Henga (Bethells).

2 Arataki Information Centre

This can provide you with details of the tracks and other features of the park. For a quick insight into the nature of the park follow the Scenic Drive between Titirangi and Swanson.

3 Muriwai Beach

Located at the northern end of the Waitakeres, Muriwai is a small community focused on the long sandy beach that extends northwards for 50 km. This is a great beach for surfing, and land yachts can be hired nearby. The 18-hole Muriwai golf course is a few minutes drive north.

4 Muriwai Gannet Colony

Just before Muriwai Beach, after descending the hill, a road goes to the left and up to a high headland, from where paragliders and hang-gliders launch themselves into the onshore winds. From the carpark a 5-minute walk will take you to the end of a high rocky outcrop overlooking a huge colony of Australasian gannets. Normally restricted to offshore islands, this is one of only three gannet breeding colonies located on a major landmass anywhere in the world. Cape Kidnappers, near Napier, is also home to a gannet colony.

5 Te Henga Walkway

This track takes you along the cliff-top and through farmland between Te Henga (Bethells) Beach and Constable Road, near Muriwai Beach. It offers great ocean

AUCKLAND

Swanson

Titirangi

Waiatarua

Arataki Information Centre

Scenic Drive

Scenic Drive

2

Huia Road

Cornwallis

ha Road

Little Huia

9

Manukau Harbour

Whatipu Beach

RANGES

views and can be walked in either direction. From Te Henga the track starts opposite the carpark for Lake Wainamu (also a nice walk). There are some steep sections, so allow 3–4 hours each way.

⑥ Goldie Bush Walkway
Also close to Muriwai Beach, this track can be combined with the Mokoroa Falls Track and Mokoroa Stream Track to make a 3-hour circuit. Moderate fitness is required for the several hilly sections. Look forward to regenerating native forest and an attractive waterfall.

⑦ Piha Beach
This is possibly the most popular beach settlement near Auckland city, and is accessed via Piha Road from Waiatarua. Swimming and surfing are the main activities but beware of the rips – they don't make a prime-time TV programme about lifesaving at Piha without good reason.

⑧ Karekare Beach
For a feeling of rugged wilderness, where spectacular Waitakere rainforest meets

the sea, visit Karekare Beach. Made famous as the opening backdrop to the Oscar-winning movie 'The Piano', access and development is carefully managed to maintain its unique, isolated character, so close to the sprawling Auckland isthmus.

⑨ Huia Road along the Southern Coast
At Titirangi turn left into Huia Road to explore the southern edge of the Waitakere Ranges Regional Park and view the Manukau Harbour. From this harbour early Maori people gathered fish and shellfish, as they continue to do today. You will find many picnic spots along this road and hiking tracks are signposted. Be sure to get a map before you start walking as many tracks intersect and resemble spaghetti in their complexity. The beaches within the harbour can provide good swimming but take care with tides as there are no lifeguards on patrol. Beyond Little Huia is an unsealed, gravel road that leads to Whatipu Beach, and the Whatipu Scientific Reserve, an important nesting area for rare species of native birdlife. The views, dunes and wetlands can be enjoyed via several tracks and are well worth the journey. Whatipu Beach is considered dangerous.

This popular summer holiday destination for Kiwis has a wonderfully rugged wilderness interior surrounded by white sandy beaches and warm Pacific Ocean. Early Maori settlements thrived on the abundant food sources, while the Europeans chased kauri timber and gold in the hills and valleys.

Gold-mining and forestry have all but disappeared, allowing nature to recover, and thus attracting visitors from all over the world for the recreational opportunities and warm climate. Fishing, arts and crafts, history and heritage, natural places with hiking opportunities galore, locally-sourced food and seafood all combine with a relaxed local lifestyle to create a special part of New Zealand. Wherever you visit, the water is only a stone's throw away.

❶ Thames Township and Attractions

Only 1.5 hours drive from Auckland, Thames is the largest town on the Peninsula. This old gold-mining town has a lot of historical interest in its buildings and museums – visit the gold-mining museums and stamping battery; and don't miss the Saturday food and crafts market. For walks try the Karaka Bird Hide boardwalk to view native birds among the mangroves, or Rocky's Goldmine Trail (3 hours). The Kauaeranga Valley in the Coromandel Forest Park has many tracks. Walk as far as you like along the Kauri trail before returning, or stay overnight at the Pinnacles Hut. Allow 8 hours for the round trip to the Pinnacles.

❷ Rapaura Water Gardens

Rapaura is a private garden of 64 acres surrounded by the Coromandel Forest Park. When exploring this garden you will encounter native and exotic flora, ponds, sculpture and lawns connected by paths and bridges. There is a restaurant and accommodation onsite. Located approximately 24 km north and inland from Thames on the Tapu-Coroglen Road. Open 9 am–5 pm daily (may vary slightly during winter).

❸ Coromandel Township and Walkway

One hour north of Thames, Coromandel township has modern cafés and craft shops occupying the historic street-front buildings preserved from gold-mining days. Scenic and fishing cruises, and guided tours depart from here. Just south of the town are the Waiau Waterworks where bike-powered water-jets, water-wheels, music boxes and flying foxes are constructed from unusual materials and powered by water to create fun-filled entertainment.

❹ Driving Creek Railway

The Driving Creek Railway was constructed through challenging terrain to source clay for a nearby pottery. Today this narrow-gauge mountain railway takes visitors on an hour-long scenic trip through native forest encountering viaducts, spirals and tunnels along the way. Located 3 km north of Coromandel township.

❺ Whitianga and Mercury Bay

Captain James Cook anchored here in 1769 to observe the transit of Mercury, hence the name. Whitianga is a great base for exploring the area with lots of accommodation options. A small ferry crosses over to Ferry Landing where shuttles

COROMANDEL PENINSULA

Firth of Thames

Tapu
2
Rapaura Water Gardens

COROMANDEL RANGE

SH25

roglen

Coromandel
3

Driving Creek Railway
4

5 Whitianga

Ferry Landing

5

Mercury Bay

7

Cathedral Cove

Matarangi

SH25

N

and tours can take you to Hot Water Beach and Cathedral Cove. Mountain-biking, cruise and diving trips also start from here.

⑥ Hahei

Gazing out at the Pacific Ocean, the small, quiet coastal village of Hahei has an enviable setting above a long white sandy beach. A general store, a few small shops and a petrol station will meet your basic needs while you focus on the beach, the sunshine and the various ways to enjoy it. Try a local sea kayaking or boat excursion along the stunning coastline, scuba dive or snorkel the marine reserve, or visit Cathedral Cove and Hot Water Beach. Dine out at the Luna Café for delicious meals in a relaxed, friendly atmosphere. The Church Café has a great menu utilising fresh ingredients from their own garden in a renovated wooden church.

⑦ Cathedral Cove and the Marine Reserve

There are two ways to reach the very beautiful Cathedral Cove – by boat, or follow a hillside track for roughly 45 minutes. You will arrive at a white sandy beach surrounded by high cliffs and pohutukawa trees. Walk through a high cave to a second beach. Swimming and sunbathing are compulsory, but be sure to bring drinking water and sunscreen. The surrounding ocean is part of Cathedral Cove Te

Whanganui-A-Hei Marine Reserve. To reach the Cathedral Cove carpark turn left after the Hahei shops. A walking track also starts from Hahei beach.

⑧ Hot Water Beach

Three minutes walk along the beach you (and a few others, it's a popular activity) will find a natural spring of hot water seeping through the sand. The water contains harmless minerals, though be sure not to drink it, and when pooled behind a wall of sand (BYO or hire a local spade) makes a fine – and free – outdoor spa. Be careful though: put your foot in the wrong spot and you will get a nasty understanding of how hot it can be. The hot springs are accessible 2 hours either side of low tide.

⑨ Tairua and Pauanui

These two small towns are well located beside safe swimming beaches. Fishing and scuba trip operators can help you explore the small offshore islands. Local walking tracks include the Broken Hills area in the Puketui Valley with relics from gold-mining days.

WAIKATO, RAGLAN & WAITOMO

The Waikato region stretches from the Coromandel to Taupo and west to the Tasman Sea. It was here that some of the largest battles between the British colonial authorities and Maori tribes occurred. Most signs of war have now disappeared and been replaced by lush, green farmland supporting massive dairy, beef and sheep industries. Meandering through the middle of the region is the Waikato River, New Zealand's longest river at 425 km.

❶ Ngaruawahia

Ngaruawahia, a small town north of Hamilton, is where the Maori King Tuheitia Paki resides at Turangawaewae Marae. The first Maori King was crowned in 1858 in an effort to unify the Maori people and stem the loss of land and resources to British authorities and settlers. Near here is Taupiri Mountain, a sacred place for burials.

❷ Hamilton Gardens

Hamilton is the largest city in the Waikato region. If passing through, visit the Botanical Gardens for enjoyable walks and picnic spots surrounded by beautiful trees and gardens of mixed exotic and native varieties.

❸ Raglan Surfing Mecca

Raglan is (for no good reason) off the radar of most travellers, except for those afflicted by the surfing bug. The surf breaks around this area attract surfers from all over New Zealand and the world. Manu Bay (Waireke) is famous for reputedly having the longest left-hand break in the world, and an international surfing competition is held here every summer. The warm climate and surfing community certainly contribute to the personality of this friendly, relaxed town. Around the town you can swim, surf, hike, fish, scuba dive and more.

❹ Mt Karioi

Mt Karioi can be climbed using the Te Toto track from the coastal road west of Raglan (3.5 hours to the top) or the Wairake Track (3 hours to the top). Panoramic 360 degree views from this extinct volcano extend as far as Mt Pirongia and even Mt Taranaki on a fine day.

❺ Bridal Veil Falls Track

Twenty km south of Raglan, this is an easy 10-minute walk to a view of the 55-metre-high Bridal Veil Falls.

❻ Aotea and Kawhia Harbours

Around these two natural harbours small communities enjoy a quiet, rural, coastal lifestyle that includes safe swimming beaches and lots of recreational opportunities. Several species of endangered, migratory birds frequent these tidal harbours and are easily observed by nature-lovers.

❼ Te Puia Hot Springs

These natural hot springs are found on Ocean Beach past Kawhia township. The springs are exposed roughly 2 hours either side of low tide. After locating a hot spot, dig a shallow hole in the black sand (with a shovel if possible) to create a natural spa. Be sure to have footwear on the beach as the black sand can itself become quite hot from the powerful sun.

❽ Pirongia Forest Park Tracks

The Pirongia Forest Park is one of the largest areas of original native forest left in the Waikato. A network of tracks provides access to the various valleys and extinct volcanic cones. The Mangakara Nature Walk takes about an hour and is relatively easy. Numbered posts indicate points of interest along the track – take a pamphlet that explains these. The Nikau track explores the virgin forest and has swimming holes and picnic spots. The track starts from Kaniwhaniwha carpark and follows a stream across farmland – allow 3 hours for the round trip. A number of other tracks of greater difficulty climb to the summit of Mt Pirongia.

❾ Waitomo Caving Trips

The Waitomo area has been synonymous with glow-worms and limestone caving trips for decades. There are many different cave systems and and a variety of caving experiences are available. Guided trips can be easy walk-through affairs, or adventurous plunges over underground waterfalls requiring wetsuits and hard-hats. All trips include the chance to learn about cave formations and the curious cave weta and glow-worms that inhabit these dark places.

❿ Otorohanga Kiwi House and Native Bird Park

This wildlife park is located in Otorohanga township, only 15 minutes from Waitomo. The nocturnal kiwi can be viewed here, along with many other wetland and rainforest bird species in large walk-through aviaries that recreate their natural habitat – it is also possible to see geckos and tuataras. Open daily between 9 am and 4.30 pm. Otorohanga also has an information centre and many services for visitors.

Huntly

Taupiri Mountain

SH1 to AUCKLAND

HAKARIMATA RANGE

1 Ngaruawahia

SH39

SH26 to
MORRINSVILLE

HAMILTON

2

SH23

SH1 to
CAMBRIDGE

Kaniwhaniwha carpark

8

PIRONGIA FOREST PARK

SH39

Mt Pirongia

Pirongia

Te Awamutu

SH31

SH39

Otorohanga **10**

Waitomo Caves **9**

SH3 to TE KUITI

ROTORUA CITY

As the earth's continents shift they cause earthquakes and volcanic eruptions – meaningless to Earth itself but potentially devastating to the people and places that encounter them. However, Rotorua takes the risks with the benefits. The people of the Te Arawa tribe arrived first and soon learnt how the hot springs and mineral pools could enhance their daily lives and traditions. Once the Europeans arrived during the mid-1800s the thermal secret was out and tourists have flocked here ever since. Thermal activity and Maori culture are Rotorua's main drawcards, with a healthy dose of trout fishing and adventure thrown in for good measure.

The reason for the town's nickname, Sulphur City, will become apparent as you drive into town – the sulphur smell is constant. Geysers, mineral pools, hot thermal springs and mud-pools are scattered within and around the city.

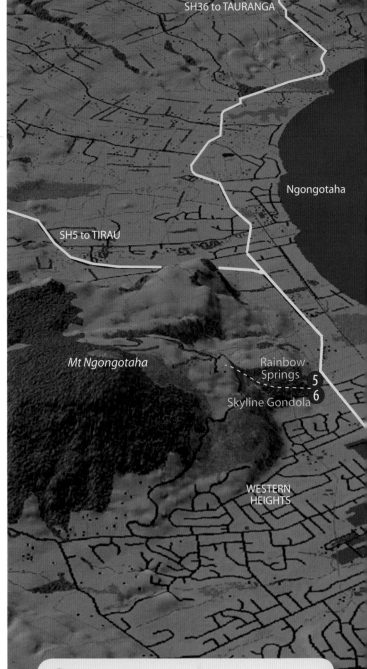

❶ Government Gardens
The Government Gardens are an essential part of anyone's visit to Rotorua. Less botanical than recreational, bowling greens and croquet lawns lie in front of the historic Bath House building. Today this building houses the Rotorua Museum of Art and History and a café. Beyond the museum you will find the Motutara golf course and then Lake Rotorua. A very pleasant walking track follows the lakeshore.

❷ Rotorua Museum of Art and History
This distinctive building was constructed as a Bath House by the New Zealand government to encourage tourism in the area. Water from thermal springs was piped to the private rooms where guests bathed and received massage and various treatments. The baths closed long ago but the rooms have been restored as much as possible for visitors to appreciate. The rest of the museum presents fascinating stories about the Te Arawa people, the renowned Pink and White Terraces, the Mt Tarawera eruption and the stories of B Company 28 Maori Battalion during WW II. The museum galleries regularly have fine-art and photographic exhibitions. Open daily, except Christmas Day, between 9 am–5 pm (8 pm October–March).

❸ Polynesian Spa
In 1878 a Catholic priest, Father Mahoney, camped here beside the lake and found the hot mineral pools much to his liking. After a few months his arthritis was cured, and the rest, as they say, is history. Today the mineral pools are open to the public, sourcing water from an incredibly hot spring nearby – so hot that it needs to be cooled with water from the town supply. The Lake Spa section has views over Lake Rotorua and offers various therapies which must be pre-booked. Open from 8 am until 11 pm daily.

❹ Te Puia and Whakarewarewa Thermal Valley
This is the most significant thermal area close to the city, and is home to New Zealand's Maori Cultural Centre, Te Puia, where students learn the art of Maori carving and weaving. Take a walk around the Whakarewarewa Thermal Valley to view the geysers, bubbling mud-pools and steaming-hot thermal water. Visit the nocturnal Kiwi House. Cultural shows are provided three times daily (and once in the evening, with a buffet dinner) to experience Maori dance, songs, weaponry and stories of the Te Arawa people. Open daily 8 am–6 pm during summer (5 pm during winter).

❺ Rainbow Springs and Kiwi Encounter
This nature park is based around a massive fresh-water spring that supports pools full of rainbow trout and a garden of native New Zealand plant and bird-life. Tuatara and kiwi can also be viewed in their secure enclosures. Open daily between 8 am and 9 pm.

❻ Skyline Gondola
Take a gondola ride up Mount Ngongotaha for tremendous views over the city and lake. At the top you will find the Luge, a three-wheeled-cart ride downhill on a concrete track. A restaurant and bar serve lunch and dinner. Open from 9 am daily until late.

❼ Kuirau Park
Kuirau Park is a stark reminder that Rotorua sits on a hotbed of thermal activity. This park in Ranolf Street features small bubbling mud-pools which are usually quiet but occasionally burst into life. (It is no surprise for some Rotorua people to wake up and find that hot mud or steam has erupted in their garden or under their house.)

❽ Fishing Trips and Cruises
With so many lakes and rivers around Rotorua, the fishing and cruising options are plentiful and varied. Local guides can take you by land or water to their favourite spots in pursuit of the wily rainbow trout. Scenic cruises operate on several lakes including Rotorua and Tarawera.

❾ Scenic Flights
Scenic flights by small plane or helicopter can show you the volcanic nature of the Rotorua region from above. Fly over or land on Mt Tarawera, Mokoia Island wildlife sanctuary and even as far as White Island off the Bay of Plenty coast.

SH33 to TE PUKE

SH30 to WHAKATANE

Mokoia Island

Lake Rotorua

Kawaha Point

9 Rotorua Airport

Motutara Point

8

OHINEMUTU

Queens Drive

7 Kuirau Park

1 Government Gardens **2** Museum of Art & History

3 Polynesian Spa

HILLCREST

Ranolf St

Fenton St

Te Ngae Road

LYNMORE

4 Te Puia Whakarewarewa Thermal Valley

WHAKAREWAREWA FOREST

SH30 to TAUPO

SH5 to TAUPO

SH33 to TE PUKE

N

Lake Rotoma

Lake Rotoehu

Lake Rotoiti

Ruato

9

10

Hells Gate
Wai Ora 3

Lake Okataina

Lake Rotorua

Lake Okareka

Lake Tikitapu
(Blue Lake)

6

SH36 to
TAURANGA

5 WHAKAREWAREWA
FOREST

Rotorua

SH5 to TIRAU

SH30 to TAUPO

New Zealand's situation on the continental plate boundary, known as the Pacific 'Ring of Fire', is demonstrated along the full length of the country. The uplifted mountains of the Southern Alps and isolated hot springs are evidence in the South Island. Scattered around the North Island are many individual volcanic cones (active, dormant and extinct), including Taranaki, Ruapehu and the many small cones around Auckland.

Rotorua's situation is quite different. The whole area, spanning hundreds of square kilometres, is a very thin, broken and fractured layer of the earth's crust. Through every fault and fissure, the heat and minerals from the underlying magma are rising to the surface, creating geysers, steaming fumaroles, oily mud-pools and hot water springs.

❶ Waimangu Volcanic Valley and Lake Rotomahana

The 1886 eruption that split Mt Tarawera in two also cracked open a 17-km-long series of craters. Waimangu Valley and Lake Rotomahana are part of this series, comprising the only hydro-thermal system in the world whose creation can be pinned down to an exact date. From the visitor centre several paths (easy or challenging) lead down the valley through regenerating native forest, passing thermal lakes large and small, silica terraces and trickling creeks laden with

minerals of many colours. After walking as far as you like (from 1–4 hours), a free shuttle can return you to the visitor centre. Transport from the city is also available. Open daily from 8.30 am–5 pm, with last admission at 3.45 pm (an hour later in January).

❷ Wai O Tapu

Walking around Wai O Tapu is a visual feast of steaming vents, misty pools, bubbling mud, and multi-coloured ground features created by various mineral deposits. The Lady Knox Geyser is another attraction, guaranteed to erupt at 10.15 am – get there early if you want to experience it. Open between 8.30 am and 5 pm daily (last admission 3.45 pm).

❸ Hell's Gate Reserve and Spa, and Wai Ora Spa

Hell's Gate geothermal reserve is 50 acres of volcanic variety – steaming fumaroles, boiling mud-pools and the cascading Kakahi Falls, reputedly the largest hot waterfall in the Southern Hemisphere. At Hell's Gate Spa and the nearby Wai Ora Spa visitors can soak in geothermal mud and sulphurous waters, in public or private baths. Massage and spa treatments are also available. Open daily between 8.30 am and 8.30 pm.

9 **Lake Okataina Walking Tracks**

To reach Lake Okataina drive along SH 30 and turn south into Okataina Road at Ruato. This scenic reserve has wonderful native forest containing rimu, rata and pohutukawa trees, and is busy with native birdlife. Walking tracks are plentiful – some easy, some more difficult – and explore the forest, a few small lakes and the larger Lake Okataina.

10 **White Water Rafting**

The rivers around Rotorua and the Central Plateau offer some of the best white-water rafting opportunities in New Zealand. The scenery is spectacular, and the variety of rivers ensures that whatever level of excitement and difficulty you are looking for can be arranged. Trips range between Grade 2 for beginners and families, right up to Grade 5 for adrenalin junkies. You may like to consider the world's highest commercially rafted waterfall. Experienced guides, equipment and full instruction are provided, and high safety standards are guaranteed. Be sure to book ahead.

4 Buried Village at Te Wairoa

The violent eruption of Mt Tarawera in 1886 buried the village of Te Wairoa in rock, mud and ash, killing 153 people in this and several other smaller villages nearby. Today, the village has been partly excavated to provide a sobering insight into the tragedy. The associated museum presents villagers' belongings and other relics recovered from the village, describing the eruption and the unique Pink and White Terraces that were also destroyed. Free 30-minute guided tours are provided at various times during the day. Between November and April a free shuttle service is available from Rotorua. Open between 9 am and 5 pm.

5 Whakarewarewa Forest

Locally known as the Redwoods, the Whakarewarewa Forest is 5 minutes drive from the centre of Rotorua. This forest was originally planted in 1901 with 170 different native and exotic tree species in an attempt to find the species with the most potential for commercial forestry. Radiata pine grew very successfully and now represents the majority of New Zealand's plantation forests. However, the stars of the forest are no doubt the Californian redwoods, towering above the rest. This forest is especially popular with mountain bikers for whom there is a network of established tracks. A nature trail and other tracks are well formed for walkers.

6 Blue Lake Reserve (Lake Tikitapu)

The Blue Lake is south-east of Rotorua along Tarawera Road and is a great place for walks, picnics, swims and various water sports. A circuit of the lake is relatively easy and takes roughly 1.5–2 hours, passing through native and exotic forest. There are good views over both the Blue and Green lakes. The final part of the circuit is back along the road.

7 Tarawera Landing

Beyond the Blue Lake, at the end of Tarawera Road you will find Lake Tarawera. The Landing is where boats depart for scenic tours of Lake Tarawera and Lake Rotomahana. A restaurant is located opposite the wharf. The culturally important Tuhourangi rock paintings can be found at Tarawera Orchard, Punaromia. Start at the gate by Tarawera Landing and follow the track for 5 minutes.

8 Mt Tarawera

Mt Tarawera was split in two during the 1886 eruption. It is privately owned, but access up the mountain is possible by joining a guided trip by 4WD. Helicopter trips are also available to fly over or land on the mountain.

LAKE TAUPO

Lake Taupo lies in the crater created by an enormous volcanic eruption around 27,000 years ago. It last erupted less than 2000 years ago, in an explosion reckoned to be the largest on earth in the past 5000 years, which was heard as far away as China. Fortunately New Zealand was uninhabited at the time, but the native flora and fauna no doubt had a rough time. Lake Taupo, New Zealand's largest lake, lies in the centre of an active volcanic area stretching from Mt Ruapehu in the south, to White Island off the Bay of Plenty coast.

1 Fishing
Rainbow trout are the main attraction here. The lake and nearby rivers have an international reputation for exciting fly fishing. Local guides can take you cruising or walking to their recommended spots, or advice is available from fishing shops and boat-hire companies.

2 Huka Falls
The Waikato River is the most significant outlet for Lake Taupo. Just north of the city the river is forced through a long, narrow 15-metre-wide channel and over a series of small waterfalls before plunging over the final 11-metre-high waterfall. The volume of water flowing through this channel and over the falls is huge – 220,000 litres per second at its peak. Huka Falls is signposted from the main road out of Taupo. Walk 3 minutes to several viewing points beside the channel.

3 Aratiatia Rapids Track
From the last viewpoint over the Huka Falls a sign indicates a track leading to a cliff-top view over the river. From here the track follows the Waikato River for 2 hours, crossing a reserve beside Lake Aratiatia before it reaches the Aratiatia Rapids, where the river flows for one kilometre through a series of small rapids.

4 Craters of the Moon
This thermal area near Taupo changed greatly when the Wairakei Power Station (2 km north) was developed over 50 years ago, diverting the underground water. Vents began to emit sulphurous steam and boiling mud-pools have become more active. The Craters of the Moon can be safely explored using the paths and boardwalks carefully placed to avoid the soft ground and steaming vents.

5 Lake Taupo Museum and Art Gallery
The outstanding feature of this museum is the '100% Pure New Zealand Ora – Garden of Well-being', which won a gold prize at the 2004 Chelsea Flower Show in London. This garden and the museum galleries provide a wonderful insight into the volcanic nature of the land, the native flora and fauna, and the traditions and legends of the central North Island region.

6 Waipahihi Botanical Reserve
This 35 ha reserve is an island of nature surrounded by humanity, close to the centre of Taupo. Exotic trees and flower gardens mix with native trees, attracting birdlife and local residents alike. Located on a hill, the stunning views encompass Lake Taupo and the distant mountains of Tongariro National Park.

7 Orakei Korako Thermal Area
The hidden valley of Orakei Korako was originally occupied by Maori, who used the hot pools for cooking. The eruption of Mt Tarawera in 1886 may have caused the people to move away from such a volcanically active place. Today the valley is visited by purchasing a ticket that includes a short river-crossing by boat to where a walking track begins. Around the valley you will encounter large silica terraces, active geysers, boiling hot springs and mud pools.

8 Jet-boats
Local jetboat operators cruise Lake Taupo and surrounding rivers exploring a variety of waterfalls (including Huka Falls) and other natural features. If you haven't experienced a 360-degree spin in a jet-boat you are missing out.

SH1 to TOKOROA, ROTORUA

Atiamuri

SH30 to WHAKAMARU

Waikato River

9 Wairakei International Golf Course
Of Taupo's five 18-hole golf courses, the Wairakei course is the best and is rated amongst the world's top 20. This championship-standard course sprawls across 450 acres of beautiful countryside. Open to the public, upon payment of green fees, every day except Christmas Day. Clubs and carts are available for hire.

10 Maori Rock Carvings at Mine Bay
The 10-metre-high Maori rock carvings at Mine Bay are visited frequently owing to their remarkable size and the obvious skill required to create such an artistic gift for the people of Taupo. They were created by master carver Matahi Whakataka-Brightwell in the late 1970s, and can only be viewed from the water. Local boat operators provide trips to see them, and can explain the significance of the figures depicted.

11 Opepe Bush Scenic and Historic Reserve
This reserve is 17 km along the Napier-Taupo highway. On the northern side of the road a 45-minute loop track leads through beautiful native forest to a graveyard where soldiers from the Bay of Plenty cavalry were buried after battling Te Kooti's rebel forces. On the southern side of the road a loop track leads to an historic logging sawpit and relics of the old Opepe township (allow 1.5 hours for the circuit).

Mine Bay 10

1

Lake Taupo

SH5 to ROTORUA

N

Lake Ohakuri

Orakei Korako 7

Ohaaki Broadlands

Waikato River

TAHORAKURI FOREST

Wairakei

3 Aratiatia Dam & rapids

Wairakei International
Golf Course 9

Waikato River

4
Craters of
the Moon

2 Huka Falls

8

Mt Tauhara

ke Taupo
Museum 5

TAUPO

6 Waipahihi Botanical Reserve

Opepe Bush 11

SH5 to NAPIER

SH1 to TURANGI

11 *White Island*

Cape Runaway

SH35

Bay of Plenty

Te Kaha

SH2 to
TAURANGA

Whakatane

SH30 to
ROTORUA

Opotiki

RAUKUMARA RANGE

SH2

Wharekopae

4 Rere
Rere Waterfall

SH38 to
MURUPARA

Gisborne

5

6

Te Urewera
National
Park

Lake Waikareiti

Kaiti Beach
Tairawhiti Musem
Te Poho-o-Rawiri
Marae

Poverty Bay

Aniwaniwa

9

10 *Onepoto Caves*

Lake Waikaremoana

Morere Springs **7**

Wairoa

SH2 to NAPIER

Mahia Beach

8 Mahia Peninsula
Scenic Reserve

*Mahia
Peninsula*

Hawke Bay

EASTLAND

A journey around the East Cape between Opotiki and Gisborne may appear to be an unfashionable diversion from the more established touring routes through the North Island. However this region provides an experience you can't get along SH 1 – remote coastal scenery, untouched wilderness, few people and small settlements free from the pressure of concrete cities and constant traffic.

Eastland has witnessed significant Maori and European historical events. The Tainui and Arawa people landed at Cape Runaway after their sea-voyage from Hawaiki more than 1000 years ago. Captain Cook and his crew landed here on 8 October 1769, the first Europeans to set foot on New Zealand soil.

Travelling between Opotiki and Gisborne may take as little as 6 hours and can therefore be done in one day. Instead, take 2 or more days and stay a night in any of the small villages around the Cape. The warm sunny climate, sandy beaches and extensive natural habitat are there to enjoy.

❶ Te Araroa
This small village has good services and accommodation options as well as the largest pohutukawa tree in New Zealand. Try the locally produced manuka honey.

❷ East Cape Lighthouse
Turn off at Te Araroa for the 22-km unsealed road to East Cape, the most easterly point on New Zealand's main islands. Take a deep breath – between you and the historic lighthouse are 700 steps.

❸ Tolaga Bay
Tolaga Bay is a small village with great beaches for swimming and fishing. Take a walk along the 660-metre pier – New Zealand's longest. To the south is a 5.5-km walk to the beautiful Cooks Cove where Captain Cook stopped to re-supply and make repairs.

❹ Rere Waterfall and Natural Rock Slide
Travel inland towards Rere and Wharekopae to reach a 60-metre-long natural rock slide, worn reasonably smooth by the flowing river. It's safe and fun to slide down on a boogie-board or inflatable mattress, but be careful. Nearby is the beautiful Rere Waterfall, a great place for swims and picnics.

❺ Gisborne City and Wineries
Gisborne city is the largest urban area in the Eastland region with over 30,000 people. A monument at Kaiti Beach on the south-eastern side of the port commemorates Captain Cook's landing. From here you can walk or drive up to viewpoints over the city and bay. The Tairawhiti Museum on Stout Street has an excellent art gallery and collections of historical artefacts. Eastland's first serious winemaking started near Gisborne in the 1920s and today there is a significant industry producing award-winning Chardonnay and Gewurztraminer.

❻ Te Poho-o-Rawiri Marae
This marae below Kaiti Hill may be the largest Maori meeting house in New Zealand. Built in 1930 with some modern features it nevertheless has wonderful examples of traditional carving and weaving. Contact the Gisborne i-Site to discuss visiting this marae. A small donation is appreciated.

❼ Morere Scenic Reserve and Hot Springs
This is a wonderful patch of native forest with various walking tracks and abundant birdlife. The hot springs are well established, with public and private pools. If staying at their accommodation, you can soak in the thermal waters after-hours. Observe the glow-worms at night.

❽ Mahia Peninsula Scenic Reserve
Drive for 7 km south of Mahia Beach (on an unsealed road) to reach the 3.5-km loop track around this reserve, with great views to the west along the Wairoa coast. Allow 2.5 hours, average fitness required.

❾ Lake Waikaremoana
Within Te Urewera National Park you will find picturesque Lake Waikaremoana and many short and multi-day tracks. The Hinerau loop track takes you to 3 waterfalls. To reach the smaller Lake Waikareiti, a gentle track (2 hours return) takes you through lush beech forest full of birdlife. The 3–4 day Great Walk around Lake Waikaremoana is reasonably undemanding and popular for its diverse scenery.

❿ Onepoto Caves Walk
South of Aniwaniwa visitor centre, where SH 38 meets Lake Waikaremoana, is the signposted track for the Onepoto Caves. Along the forested track you can explore many caves (take a torch to avoid hazards), tunnels and rocky overhangs. There are some steep sections, so allow 2 hours for the return trip.

⓫ White Island
White Island is an active volcano located 48 km north of Whakatane in the Bay of Plenty. Constantly steaming and bubbling, and sometimes releasing mud, lava and ash, White Island attracts vulcanologists from around the world. It is possible to visit the island during a 6-hour cruise from Whakatane, or by helicopter from Whakatane or Rotorua.

Hicks Bay
Te Araroa ❶
❷ East Cape
Ruatoria
Tokomaru Bay
Tolaga Bay ❸
N

TONGARIRO

Waiouru **7**
Army Museum

Desert Road

Tongariro Northern Circuit **2**

SH1 to TURANGI

1

Turangi

Mt Ngauruhoe

Mt Tongariro

Mangetepopo Valley

2

Tongariro
Alpine Crossing

SH46 to
RANGIPO

Ketetahi

Tongariro National Park contains the most active volcanic mountains on mainland New Zealand. Located just south of Lake Taupo, Mts Ruapehu, Tongariro and Ngauruhoe rise up from the central plateau. Mt Ngauruhoe is actually the main vent for Mt Tongariro with its most recent eruption occurring in 1973. Ruapehu is also active and has a reputation for lahars – a flood or flow of volcanic mud and debris collected as it rushes downhill.

In 1887 the people of the Ngati Tuwharetoa tribe gifted these mountains to the nation and they became New Zealand's first national park (and only the fourth in the world). In 1990 Tongariro National Park was given World Heritage status for its outstanding natural values and in 1993 its cultural values were also recognised. The mountains provide year-round adventures – hiking in the summer, skiing in the winter. The mountains are complemented by lakes, rivers and untouched native forest making this national park a fascinating and exciting destination for visitors.

1 Turangi and Trout Fishing
Turangi at the southern end of Lake Taupo is a small town renowned for the excellent trout fishing and white water rafting opportunities nearby.

2 Tongariro Alpine Crossing and Tongariro Northern Circuit
Requiring up to 9 hours, covering 17 km and climbing over 900 metres, the Tongariro Alpine Crossing, negotiates the saddle between Mts Ngauruhoe and Tongariro. Starting from the Mangatepopo Valley end will reduce the amount of climbing required. The volcanic landscape is unique in New Zealand. The Northern Circuit is one of New Zealand's 'Great Walks' and is comfortably done in 4 days. Good fitness is required for both walks on the exposed, challenging terrain, and you must be equipped for all types of weather. The scenery is spectacular, with alpine plants, old lava flows, emerald-coloured lakes, mountain springs and volcanic rock. The weather on the mountain can change quickly at any time of year so it is essential to be well prepared with wet-weather gear, food and water. Booking ahead is recommended for both walks, as is checking conditions with local information centres.

3 Whakapapa Village
The tiny Whakapapa Village is a destination in its own right, and with plenty of accommodation, restaurants and other services (including gear-hire) it's a great place to base yourselves while enjoying the surrounding natural attractions. Visit

Map labels:
SH1 to TAIHAPE
Tangiwai
SH49
Mt Ruapehu
Ohakune
6
5 Turoa Skifield
4 Mangawhero Falls
5
4
Tukino Skifield
SH4 to RAETIHI
Whakapapa Skifield
5
Hauhangatahi
Whakapapa Village
3
SH48
National Park
SH4 to TAUMARANUI
SH47
Whakapapa River
TONGARIRO FOREST

the iconic Chateau Tongariro for a meal, accommodation, or game of golf. Around the village are various walking tracks that will take you 15-40 minutes, or all day if you desire. More details from the DOC visitor centre in the village.

4 Lord of the Rings Film Sites
The volcanic landscape and sharp rock formations in Tongariro National Park were used for filming locations in The Lord of the Rings movie trilogy, such as Mordor, Mount Doom and Gollum's Pool. Mangawhero Falls was the site of Ithilien Camp. Guided tours are available.

5 Local Skifields
Mt Ruapehu has 2 commercial skifields – Turoa and Whakapapa, nervously co-existing with the active volcano inside the mountain. Whakapapa is New Zealand's largest ski area. Both fields have slopes for all skill levels, cafés, equipment rental and ski schools. There are many chairlifts to the main trails and also a selection of off-piste areas. Tukino is a club-operated field on the eastern side of Mt Ruapehu. Open to the public, Tukino has 2 rope tows, ski and snowboard schools, volunteer ski patrols and some accommodation.

6 Mountain Biking, Rafting, Canoeing, Kayaking
With so much stunning wilderness it is no surprise that lovers of outdoor activities are well catered for. Bring your own gear or hire it locally; get out there independently or with a guide. The scenery ranges from bush-fringed rivers to barren exposed mountain-tops, with a variety of terrain inbetween. Information and brochures are available from DOC and Visitor Information Centres, and many cafés and accommodation places. As always, booking ahead will help to avoid delays and disappointment.

7 Waiouru Army Museum
This museum commemorates the history of the New Zealand army and relates the personal stories of individual soldiers during campaigns around the world. Memorabilia and collections of weapons and medals are displayed inside, while outside, restored military vehicles and guns guard the building. Waiouru is also the location for a major army base and training area.

NAPIER & HASTINGS

Napier and Hastings, in the Hawke's Bay region, is where winemaking began – at least in New Zealand. And they certainly have taken the grape seriously, producing our best red wine, with the assistance of copious quantities of sunshine. The Hawke's Bay recipe: take a little wine (okay, a lot), add a variety of fresh local food including olives and organic options, combine it all with a barbecue under the hot, hot sun and what have you got? A lifestyle that is very, very good.

For nearly 900 years local Maori had this glorious area to themselves. Captain James Cook sailed past in 1769, followed by temporary European visitors such as whalers. Farming began in 1848 and not long after, in 1851, French missionaries arrived. Within a few years they had planted the first vines for what has become today a huge and successful export industry.

Apart from the wineries, take advantage of the other interesting features of the region: explore the Art Deco and Spanish Mission architecture, visit the beaches, observe some wildlife, pick fresh strawberries and eat lots of ice-cream.

❶ Art Deco Napier Guided Walk

A major earthquake in 1931 devastated Napier city and killed hundreds of people. Reconstruction in the Art Deco and Spanish Mission style has created New Zealand's largest collection of such architecture. Guided tours are the best way to appreciate the history and features of the buildings. Visit the Art Deco Shop in Tennyson Street to learn about the walking tours, which depart twice daily. Tours by vehicle also visit some impressive buildings on the city outskirts.

❷ Bluff Hill Lookout

Bluff Hill can't be mistaken, it's the only hill in town. The view from the top includes the beaches, the distant horizon and the Port of Napier. Finding your way to the top can be a challenge so be sure to get a good street map.

❸ Hawke's Bay Museum

This museum presents the Bay's natural history, art, heritage and culture through Maori stories and artwork, accounts from survivors of the 1931 earthquake, and a huge number of eclectic collections with thousands of objects.

❹ The National Aquarium

The National Aquarium is situated on Marine Parade in Napier and has a reef tank; a travelator which spirals its way beneath the enormous oceanarium, creating the impression of a true underwater experience; and a typical New Zealand rocky shore environment. There are sharks, stingray and hundreds of fish species, a crocodile and some kiwis on display. Feeding times are 10 am and 2 pm.

❺ Hawke's Bay Gourmet

Hawke's Bay is a food-lover's paradise. Try a cheese tasting at Te Mata Cheese; view the busy bees at Arataki Honey's fascinating visitor centre; and indulge in strawberries and ice-cream at Rush Munro's – New Zealand's oldest ice-cream maker. Take a trip to Silky Oak Chocolate Company for a manuka honey truffle, halfway between Napier and Hastings. There's also a Farmer's Market held every weekend 8.30 am to 12.30 pm (Saturdays at the Daily Telegraph building, Tennyson St, Napier; Sundays at the Hawke's Bay Showgrounds, Hastings) and a Village Grower's Market every Saturday from 9 am to noon at Black Barn Vineyard, Havelock North.

❻ Cape Kidnappers Gannet Sanctuary

You don't need to be a committed birdwatcher to find this gannet colony impressive. Hundreds of these beautiful, if a little noisy, birds nest together on the cliff-edge of Cape Kidnappers. This is the largest mainland gannet colony in the world, best viewed between November and February. It is possible to walk to the colony by leaving your car at Clifton Domain, then walking 8 km. Be sure to check with information centres about tide times and safety. Guided tours travel overland or via the beach.

❼ Wineries

Maps showing the location and opening hours of the various wineries are widely available for self-drive exploring. Otherwise join a guided winery tour that can include wine-tasting. Many wineries also have excellent on-site restaurants and cafés set in beautiful gardens.

❽ Te Mata Peak Walkway and Lookout

Take a trip up the steep and winding road to Te Mata Peak (399 m) for the best views of Hawke's Bay, including Cape Kidnappers, Napier, Hastings and the Mahia Peninsula. Bike, drive, or hike…

❾ Ocean and Waimarama Beaches

Beyond Te Mata Peak and over a few more hills you will find these long, sandy beaches. Both are popular for walking, surfing, picnics and safe swimming. Waimarama also has a small store, fuel station, boat ramp and holiday homes for rent.

❿ Puketitiri and Mangatutu Walks and Hot Springs

Venture inland beyond Puketitiri to find several small scenic reserves and the Kaweka Forest Park, where you can explore the Mangatutu and Mangatainoka hot springs, lots of walking tracks and picnic spots.

KAWEKA FOREST PARK

10 Mangatainoka Hot Springs

SH5 to TAUPO

10 Mangatutu Hot Springs

Mohaka River

10 Puketitiri

SH50 to TAKAPAU

SH2 to WOODVILLE, WAIRARAPA

SH2 to WAIROA

Lake Tutira

Hawke Bay

2 *Bluff Hill*
3 **4** Hawke's Bay Museum
National Aquarium
Art Deco Shop

1

NAPIER

Tutaekuri River

Silky Oak Chocolate **5**

Ngaruroro River

7

Clifton

*Cape
Kidnappers*

6

Rush Munro **5**

HASTINGS

5 Arataki Honey

5 Te Mata Cheese

HAVELOCK NORTH

Grower's Market **5**

Te Mata Peak **8**

9 *Ocean Beach*

Tukituki River

9 Waimarama

N

WELLINGTON

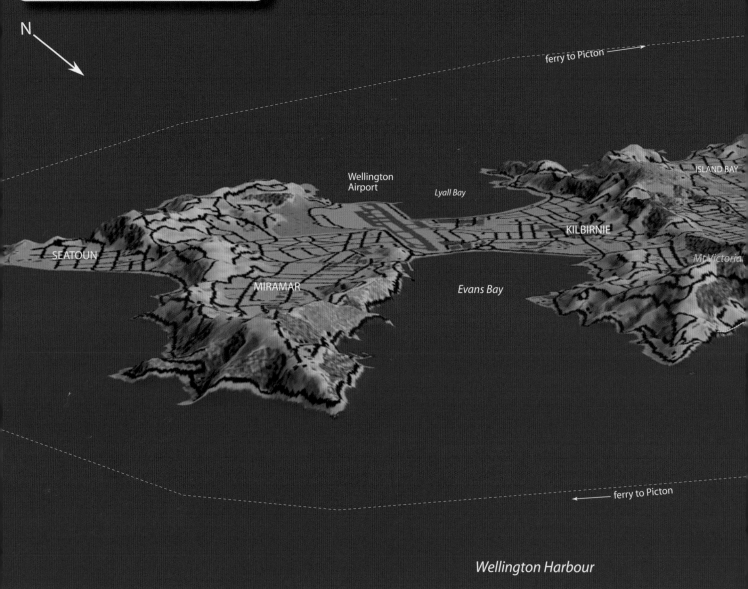

Cook Strait

N

Wellington Airport

Lyall Bay

ISLAND BAY

Wellington Airport

KILBIRNIE

SEATOUN

Mt Victoria

MIRAMAR

Evans Bay

Wellington Harbour

ferry to Picton

ferry to Picton

Wellington's precarious location on a major fault line has surprisingly contributed to its architectural character and easy walk-ability. Squeezed between the surrounding hills and a beautiful harbour, the central business and shopping districts are compact and easily explored on foot. Park your car, put on some comfortable shoes and go urban-hiking downtown to soak up the capital city's energy and atmosphere. From one of the high vantage points, such as Mt Victoria or the Cable Car's upper terminus, take a look around at the old wooden houses clinging to the hillsides, full of character and built to withstand the not infrequent earthquakes that shake the city.

Wellington is the nation's political capital and also has some of our most significant cultural and heritage attractions. Te Papa Tongarewa (The Museum of New Zealand) could easily consume a whole day, while the evenings can be filled with a vibrant mix of theatre, music and dance.

❶ The Museum of New Zealand Te Papa Tongarewa
The national museum conserves and displays our most valuable historical and cultural artefacts. Te Papa ('Our Place') is a thoroughly modern museum. The various galleries present New Zealand's natural forces and ecology, the history of human settlement, Maori culture, art collections and more. Open daily between 10 am and 6 pm, and until 9 pm on Thursdays. Free entry.

❷ Museum of Wellington City and Sea
This museum tells the tales of Wellington: the original Maori settlements, European immigration, the 1968 Wahine ferry disaster, capital city status – all in a restored heritage building. Located at Queens Wharf. Open daily between 10 am and 5 pm. Free entry.

❸ Parliament Buildings
Parliament Buildings can be explored during a free one-hour guided tour departing every hour when open. Open weekdays from 10 am–4 pm, Saturdays 10 am–3 pm, Sundays 12 pm–3 pm, closed most public holidays.

❹ Government Buildings Historic Reserve
This historic building (built 1876) appears to be constructed from stone but is actually made of wood from the native kauri tree. Explore the foyer, grand staircase and hallowed halls. Open weekdays between 9 am and 4.30 pm and Saturdays from 10 am–3 pm.

❺ Old St Paul's Cathedral
Built in 1866 from floor to ceiling in native timber, with wonderful stained-glass windows. Located in Mulgrave Street. Open daily between 10 am and 5 pm.

Labels on map: WTOWN, BROOKLYN, Karori Wildlife Sanctuary (12), KARORI, Cable Car Museum, Cable Car (9), Tinakori Hill, Courtenay Place (11), 7, 1 Te Papa Tongarewa, 10 Botanic Gardens, Oriental Bay, 2, Museum of City and Sea, Queens Wharf, 4, 6 5 3, Parliament Buildings, WADESTOWN, Old St Paul's Cathedral, Government Buildings Historic Reserve, Backbencher Pub, KHANDALLAH, SH1

6 Backbencher Pub

Mentioned here for its cultural relevance of course, the Backbencher, located conveniently opposite Parliament Buildings on Molesworth Street, has long been the watering hole of the nation's politicians. Examine the political satire around the walls expressed in entertaining puppet and cartoon form.

7 Harbour Waterfront Walk: Queens Wharf–Oriental Bay

This urban walk has it all – harbour views, history, art, sculpture, cafés, Te Papa Museum, and excellent people-watching opportunities. Begin at Queens Wharf and follow the shoreline past Te Papa and around to Oriental Bay. A detailed map is available from the visitor centre and railway station.

8 Mt Victoria

On the eastern side of the central business district is the 196-metre-high hill called Mt Victoria. From the top you have 360-degree views of the city and harbour.

9 Cable Car

The lower terminus of Wellington's Cable Car can be found down the narrow Cable Car Lane about 200 metres from the southern end of Lambton Quay. At the top (after three mid-stations and three tunnels) you will find the Botanic Gardens and the Cable Car Museum.

10 Botanic Gardens

These very enjoyable gardens can be accessed from the upper terminus of the Cable Car, or the Glenmore Street entrance. Inside are rambling paths exploring the 25 ha of native and exotic forest and plant species lovingly nurtured since 1868. Various artistic and sculptural pieces either blend or contrast nicely with their surroundings.

11 Courtenay Place

Courtenay Place is the heart of Wellington's restaurant and entertainment scene. Cuisine of every variety is available in a city that claims more restaurants, bars and cafés per person than New York. Entertainment options include the national orchestra, ballet and opera, and several independent, professional theatre companies.

12 Karori Wildlife Sanctuary

This world-first sanctuary for native birds, bats and tuatara was made possible by constructing a predator-proof fence around the perimeter. Explore by yourselves, join a short daytime tour or listen for kiwi during a sunset tour. Open daily, except Christmas Day, 10 am–5 pm, later for sunset tours.

D'Urville Island

French Pass

9

Pelorus Sound

Pelorus Sound

A quick geology lesson. The Marlborough Sounds started off as regular river valleys above sea level. The Sounds were then flooded by the ocean at tectonic speed as the Pacific Plate was slowly subducted beneath the Indo-Australian Plate. Today the long waterways and secluded coves of the Marlborough Sounds are the playground for water-lovers of every variety. Fishing folk cast their line, kayakers explore the less accessible coves, while scuba divers explore the silent shipwrecks below. As for the landlubbers, they hike along bush and beach-edged tracks in a region that boasts some of the highest sunshine hours in New Zealand.

A taste of the Sounds can be had during a one-day cruise or day-walk, but with budget and luxury accommodation options generously spread around (some best accessed by boat) a 3–6 day sojourn is a pleasant escape from the world. Be sure to enjoy a bottle or two of Marlborough's excellent wines after a hard day's exploring – great for washing down the locally grown salmon and green-lipped mussels.

1

Havelock

SH6 to RAI VALLEY, NELSON   SH6 to BLENHEIM

❶ Transport and Cruises into the Sounds
Water taxi, helicopter and float-plane operators can transfer you around the Sounds to accommodation and points along the Queen Charlotte Track with ease. Booked in connection with a hike, water taxis can transfer backpacks while you walk. Cruise operators also offer variously themed cruise activities such as fishing or nature trips, which are discussed in more depth below. Locations within Pelorus and Kenepuru sounds can be reached using water taxis from Havelock.

❷ Queen Charlotte Track
Along the 71 km of this track you will experience a wonderful variety of vegetation and views, with a mixture of coastline and hilltop sections. The track is described as a 4-day 'long, not steep' adventure, but you can day-walk sections of the track with water taxi transfers. You will need above-average fitness and a good pair of hiking boots. Most people walk from Ship Cove back to Anakiwa, staying at lodges, backpackers or DOC campsites along the way, and there are also some small shops where you can buy supplies. If you prefer to travel light, water taxis can transfer your luggage while you carry only a day-pack.

❸ Picton Walks
Close to central Picton are several walks to try, with native bush and great views. The Tirohanga walkway from Newgate Street requires 45 minutes of uphill walking to reach the Hilltop viewpoint looking over Picton. For a 2-hour round trip continue on down to Garden Terrace, where you can also try the Essons Valley walks to Humphries or Barnes dams (easy going, allow 45 minutes one way for each dam track). The Victoria Domain has a good network of easy tracks of varying duration. More details are available from the Information Centre.

❹ Queen Charlotte Scenic Drive
This scenic drive is the 35-km stretch of road between Picton and Havelock. You won't save time driving this way as the road meanders around the coastline and through native forest, but the slow speed allows you to enjoy the expansive views of Queen Charlotte and Pelorus sounds.

❺ Mountain Biking and Sea Kayaking
The Queen Charlotte Track has been designed for mountain biking as well as hiking.

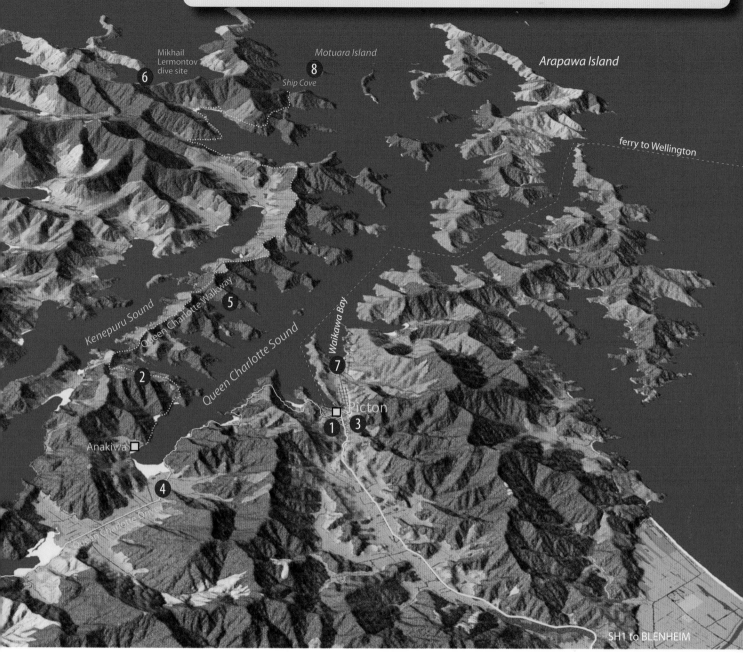

MARLBOROUGH SOUNDS & PICTON

Mikhail Lermontov dive site

⑥

Motuara Island

⑧

Ship Cove

Arapawa Island

ferry to Wellington

Kenepuru Sound

Queen Charlotte Walkway

⑤

Queen Charlotte Sound

Waikawa Bay

②

⑦

Picton

① ③

Anakiwa ☐

④

Queen Charlotte Drive

SH1 to BLENHEIM

A good level of riding is required to deal with the track conditions and slopes. There are guided and independent bike-rental options available. If you prefer to give your legs a rest, sea kayaking is a good way to work on your upper-body fitness and get closer to the marine environment and the prolific wildlife in the Sounds. Again, there are guided trips available and independent kayak-hire options (for people with some experience).

⑥ Scuba dive for Shipwrecks and Dinner
With a coastline this long and varied you know the underwater world is going to be spectacular. Local dive operators know where to find shellfish and lobster, observe the fish, and of course – the big drawcard – the Mikhail Lermontov, a 155-metre Russian cruise ship that sank here in 1986. Other wrecks are available to explore and diving gear and lessons can be provided.

⑦ Yachts and Launches for Hire
A great way to make the most of such a stunning playground is by hiring a yacht or launch to explore the many sheltered bays and water-based activities. With sufficient boating experience you can be your own skipper, or you can hire an experienced local to host you. Most boat-hire operators will have a network of private moorings, fishing and scuba gear for you to hire. You can even learn to sail as you go along. Vessels come in different shapes and sizes to suit your party.

⑧ Motuara Island
The very small Motuara Island is at the entrance to Queen Charlotte Sound. Captain Cook claimed the South Island for the Crown by raising the Union Jack flag on this island. Launch operators from Picton take nature cruises along the sound to the island where you have the chance to explore and get close to the abundant birdlife.

⑨ French Pass
French Pass is reached via a long but scenic drive branching off SH 6 at Rai Valley. Here you will find Sea Safaris, a conservation-dedicated operator introducing people to the area's Maori and European history, seals, dolphins, penguins and other seabird species.

Marlborough was a late starter in the wine game, with the first vines being planted in the 1970s, but has now overtaken Hawke's Bay as the largest wine-producing region in the country, with more than 10,400 ha planted. Compared to France and other old-world wine regions this is still tiny. However, acreage is less important than quality and it is the quality of Marlborough's wines that stands out. Wines from here, as well as elsewhere in New Zealand, have gathered awards and plaudits from around the world, especially for the Sauvignon Blancs.

① Winery Tours

Each year an updated map of the Marlborough wine region is produced showing the location of the wineries. On the back of the map are comprehensive details about each winery: wine varieties, opening hours, contact details, availability of wine sales, tastings and restaurants. This is an essential accessory for making the most of your wine-tasting day.

If you can watch others enjoy wine-tasting without envy then self-drive winery visits are possible. Otherwise join a guided winery tour. There are several operators providing this service with day or half-day options including wine and gourmet food. You can join a small group or arrange a private tour customised to suit your tastebuds. Your guides will introduce you to the interesting history of this wine region.

② Blenheim

Blenheim is the largest town in the region with a population of 28,000. The Marlborough Museum at Brayshaw Park preserves and presents the region's history (open daily except Good Friday and Christmas Day between 10 am and 4 pm). The Millennium Art Gallery on Seymour Street displays collections of local, national and visiting international artworks (open Monday–Friday 10.30 am–4.30 pm, weekends 1 pm–4 pm).

③ Nature Tours

Despite the drainage of Marlborough's wetlands and small lakes in the past, a good variety of birdlife manages to survive along the braided Wairau River and in the wetlands and tidal lagoons along the coastline near Blenheim. A loop track at the end of Hardings Road explores the lagoon. Driftwood Eco-tours take privately guided trips to look for some of the 90 bird species seen here and to view other landscapes and wildlife around the region. Each trip can be personalised by adding art, photography, wine or kayaking to make the perfect day out.

④ Whites Bay

Whites Bay is the best beach for swimming near Blenheim. The sandy beach is safe for swimming and has regenerating native bush for a backdrop. The 10-minute

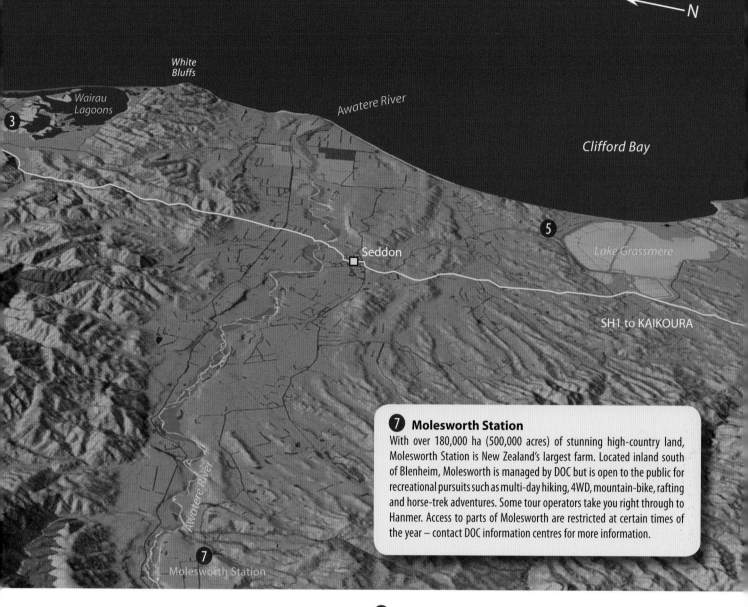

Cloudy Bay

N

White Bluffs

Wairau Lagoons

3

Awatere River

Clifford Bay

5

Seddon

Lake Grassmere

SH1 to KAIKOURA

Awatere River

7

Molesworth Station

7 Molesworth Station

With over 180,000 ha (500,000 acres) of stunning high-country land, Molesworth Station is New Zealand's largest farm. Located inland south of Blenheim, Molesworth is managed by DOC but is open to the public for recreational pursuits such as multi-day hiking, 4WD, mountain-bike, rafting and horse-trek adventures. Some tour operators take you right through to Hanmer. Access to parts of Molesworth are restricted at certain times of the year – contact DOC information centres for more information.

Pukatea walk takes you to the site of the first telegraph cable across Cook Strait. The 30-minute Black Jack Track climbs a hill to a lookout over the bay. From Blenheim, drive north towards Picton then turn right at Tuamarina for Rarangi. Follow the narrow, winding road for a few minutes towards Port Underwood.

5 Lake Grassmere Solar Salt Works

South of Blenheim in Clifford Bay are the Lake Grassmere Solar Salt Works. Evaporation of sea water by sun and wind allows the salt to be collected when it crystallises on the bottom of concentration ponds. This is a 6-month process between October and March every year. The pink colour is caused by two things: micro-algae producing a red pigment (as in the Red Sea), and tiny red shrimps.

6 Herzog Winery, Bistro and Restaurant

There are many wineries and a good selection of restaurants in this region. The risk when naming one is that perhaps we should name them all, but there isn't space to do that. However, Herzog stands apart as more than a regular restaurant. Herzog is a luxury food and wine experience, with Michelin-star European chefs, award-winning gourmet cuisine, a 22-page international wine list, dedicated personal service and cooking lessons, all set amongst a beautiful Mediterranean garden.

8 Makana Handmade Chocolates

Despite chocolate being a completely non-essential food item, it does keep a certain gender happy, so drop into the Makana Confections shop for supplies. Chocolates with nuts and fruit, truffles with sherry or lemon, chocolate macadamias, biscotti…mmmm. Located on the corner of Rapaura and O'Dwyers Road, about 10 minutes north of Blenheim. Open 7 days between 9 am and 5.30 pm, closed Christmas Day and Boxing Day.

9 Wither Hills Farm Park

The Wither Hills Farm Park occupies 1100 ha of Marlborough District Council land on the southern side of Blenheim. Open to the public, there are 50 km of walking and mountain biking tracks (some shared, many walking-only) exploring the ridges and valleys. Vegetation is sparse but the views of Blenheim and the winery region are mouth-watering. More details are available from information centres. Take a picnic and a sunhat.

NELSON CITY

RICHMOND RANGE

Dun Mountain

Pelorus River

BRYANT RANGE

N

SH6 to BLENHEIM

Wakapuaka

Cable Bay Walkway 9

Glenduan

Cable Bay

Nelson city is the commercial centre for the Nelson/Tasman region, regularly basking in the highest number of sunshine hours anywhere in New Zealand. All that good weather is not Nelson's only blessing though. Golden sandy beaches, three national parks and a multitude of recreational opportunities make this region an outdoor-lover's heaven. It is perhaps only because of its location well away from SH 1, the main holiday highway down the east coast, that Nelson has not yet been swamped by mass tourism. Nature, culture, cafés and crafts – all can be found in and around the urban area. As Horatio said, 'Live the day'!

❶ Boulder Bank
A special Nelson feature is the Boulder Bank, a 13-km long spit made up of large stones, eroded from cliffs further along the coast, and deposited by ocean currents. There are only a few of these natural formations in the world. The Boulder Bank originally stretched all the way to Haulashore Island, but 'The Cut' was made to allow greater shipping into Port Nelson. You can drive to the Boulder Bank via Wakapuaka at the northern end of the city.

❷ Queens Gardens and Suter Art Gallery
A pleasant picnic spot, with duck ponds and a variety of exotic trees and ornamental gardens. Beside the gardens on Bridge Street is the Suter Art Gallery, housing works by artists from Nelson and around New Zealand. The Suter Café has wonderful food including vegetarian options.

❸ Nelson Market
Every Saturday between 8 am and 1 pm, Nelsonians descend on Montgomery Square for crafts, food, fresh produce and buskers.

❹ Centre of New Zealand (Botanical Hill)
Take a look at a New Zealand map and you'll see why Nelson lays claim to being the centre of New Zealand. Is it really the centre? No, but this small hill close to downtown Nelson provides an enjoyable 20–30 minute uphill walk for a great view. Start from the Botanical Reserve at the end of Hardy Street.

❺ Nelson Cathedral
Walk up the steps of Church Hill to reach Nelson Cathedral, completed in 1965 using marble from the Takaka Hill. Open to the public, the surrounding gardens are a pleasant picnic spot.

❻ The Grampians
Overlooking the city are the Grampians, high hills with several walking tracks providing great views of the surrounding valleys and across to Kahurangi National Park. Start walking from downtown or park a little closer. The track begins from Fairfield House at the top of Trafalgar Street or from the top of Collingwood Street. It's fairly steep, so allow an hour to reach the top, where a viewing platform awaits.

The Grampians

Nelson 6

Botanical Hill (Centre of NZ)
Queens Gardens, Suter Art Gallery

Cathedral
Nelson Market

4

2 5
3

10

Rocks Road

Haulashore Is.

8

1 Boulder Bank

7 Tahunanui
Beach

Stoke

World of WearableArt
Museum

10

Nelson Airport

Waimea Estuary

Tasman Bay

Richmond

SH6 to
ST ARNAUD, WEST COAST

Grape Escape
Eyebright

11

Höglunds

12

Waimea River

SH60 to
MOTUEKA

Rabbit Island

Rabbit Island
Beach

13

Waimea Estuary

14
Mapua

7 Tahunanui Beach

Tahunanui Beach is only 5 minutes drive along Rocks Road from central Nelson. A fantastic swimming beach and great for walking, jogging and people-watching.

8 Sailing Trips from Nelson

With a great climate and a stunning coastline Nelson is a great place for a nautical adventure. Several yacht and launch operators provide half-day, day or multi-day trips between Nelson, Abel Tasman and the Marlborough Sounds for cruising, fishing, scuba diving and even sailing lessons.

9 Cable Bay Walkway

Cable Bay can be reached by road 20 km to the north-east of Nelson. From there or from the Glen (Glenduan, 13 km north, at the end of the Boulder Bank) the Cable Bay Walkway explores the hillside farmland and native forest above Tasman Bay. Suitable for reasonably fit people, allow 3–3.5 hours each way and expect some uphill sections. Dogs are not permitted.

10 World Of WearableArt and Classic Cars Museum

This purpose-designed museum has two separate parts. The first gallery displays the unique garments created for the annual Nelson-inspired WOW awards and show – in sections such as Shades of White, Avant Garde, Bizarre Bras and Man Unleashed! The second gallery houses a private collection of more than 50 vehicles, classic cars from yesteryear as well as relatively modern examples.

11 Grape Escape and Eyebright

On McShane Road near Richmond are two enjoyable countryside shopping attractions. The Grape Escape has a lunch café surrounded by a garden, winery, gift shop, boutique distillery outlet and creative candles. Eyebright offers pottery, contemporary art, furniture, dried and silk flowers, jewellery and Christmas decorations.

12 Höglund Art Glass – International Glass Centre

For those who appreciate the beauty of art-glass and the skills of highly-trained glass artists, this gallery and working studio located in Lansdowne Road will not disappoint. Entry to the galleries is free, but a charge applies for a tour of the workshop with glass-blowing demonstration.

13 Rabbit Island Beach

This beach is a little removed from the city, making it quieter but still good for swims, walks and barbecues.

14 Mapua

Mapua is a cosy little village 30 minutes from Nelson at the western entrance to the Waimea estuary. Boasting several of the best cafés and restaurants in the region, you can also find gift shops, art and craft galleries and an aquarium. The Waimea estuary is an important habitat for many migratory bird species which can be seen during locally operated nature cruises.

KAHURANGI NATIONAL PARK

Karamea

Mt Arthur
6

TABLELANDS

5

Cobb
Reservoir

Mt Arthur Hut

Lodestone

Flora Carpark

Motueka River

Moutere River

Motueka
Airport

8

SH60 to NELSON

Port Motueka

Motueka

1 2

Motueka Coastal Walk

Staples St

3

N →

SH60 to TAKAKA

Riwaka
Resurgence
7

Riwaka River

4

Kaiteriteri

MOTUEKA & KAHURANGI

Motueka is a popular jumping-off point for the Abel Tasman and Kahurangi national parks. Between Motueka township and the Kahurangi wilderness the low hills, valleys and plains of the Moutere and Motueka area are bursting with vineyards and orchards, art and crafts, cafés and boutique food-producers. For a great day out buy some fresh local bread, olives, sheep cheese and other deli delights for a picnic in the great outdoors, or try a little wine-tasting before lunching at a vineyard café. Take a walk in the bush, swim in the sea, then recover with a professional massage. It's a lifestyle that fits well with the Top of the South climate and relaxed way of life.

1 Motueka
This small town of 12,000 people has a pretty relaxed pace with nice little cafés and a quirky little independent cinema. For those heading into the national parks, all the supplies and gear you may need are available here. Various transport operators provide transfers to most tracks. On Sunday mornings a food and craft market springs up behind the Information Centre.

2 Hot Mama's Café
Hot Mama's café at the northern end of Motueka has a relaxed and friendly atmosphere characteristic of the region's laid-back hippy community. Go for the alternative music, friendly service and delicious food including vegetarian dishes.

3 Motueka Coastal Walk
Motueka has a special place for birdlife right on its doorstep. The Motueka Coastal Walk follows the foreshore for an hour (one way) between Staples Street and Wharf Road. From this flat, easy track you can enjoy the beach, ocean views and tidal inlet, observing a seasonal variety of shorebirds including oystercatchers, godwits, terns and shags. The Motueka Sandspit can be explored near Staples Street, but please keep your distance from nesting birds.

4 Kaiteriteri Beach
Perhaps the most popular beach in the Nelson region, with golden sand, clear blue water and of course ice-cream, pizza and café food on demand. There are several walks through native forest not far away. You can also begin your Abel Tasman National Park adventures from here by water taxi, sea kayak or sailing catamaran.

5 Kahurangi National Park
With 452,000 ha of land, Kahurangi is New Zealand's second largest national park, occupying most of the north-west corner of the South Island. This park was created in 1996, after its incredible variety of habitats, unique wildlife and complex geology were recognised. A multitude of tracks are available for day and multi-day walks, with varying degrees of difficulty and duration: Heaphy (4–6 days, 82 km); Wangapeka (3–5 days, 52 km); Leslie/Karamea (3–4 day connection between the Tablelands and Wangapeka). Walk them independently or join a guided trip.

6 Mt Arthur and the Tablelands
This area of Kahurangi National Park is the most accessible from Motueka. An hours drive up to the Flora carpark opens up a raft of options. Walk gently downhill following a stream to Flora Hut (30 minutes one way). Follow a ridgeline track to Mt Arthur Hut (1.5 hours one way). Continue past the hut, following an exposed marked route up to Mt Arthur summit (another 3 hours one way) for fantastic views in all directions. The Mt Lodestone circuit takes you to Flora Hut then steeply uphill for equally awesome views before descending directly to the carpark (allow 4.5 hours for the circuit).

7 Riwaka Resurgence
After driving to the end of Riwaka Valley Road, an easy 5-minute walk takes you to an unusual sight – a river emerging from the hillside. This is where the clean, cold waters of the north branch of the Riwaka River emerge from a limestone cave after flowing underground for miles. Adventurous scuba divers sometimes explore the lower reaches of the cave system.

8 Sky Diving and Scenic Flights from Motueka Airport
From this busy little airport the adventurous person within you can try hang-gliding, microlights and sky diving. More relaxed flight options include transfers to Awaroa Lodge in the Abel Tasman National Park, or either end of the Heaphy Track; and scenic flights around Golden Bay, Kahurangi National Park, and several Lord of the Rings filming locations.

ABEL TASMAN & GOLDEN BAY

KAHURANGI NATIONAL PARK

Heaphy Track 11

WAKAMARAMA RANGE

15

Anatoki River

Waingaro River

Pupu Springs

10

Takaka River

8 Takaka

7 Harwoods Hole

Takaka Hill

SH60 to MOTUEKA

ABEL TASMAN NATIONAL PARK

1 Marahau

2

5

Abel Tasman Coast Track

3

4 Awaroa Lodge

6

Tonga Island Marine Reserve

Abel Tasman National Park is New Zealand's smallest but perhaps most popular national park. The golden sandy beaches, tidal estuaries, native forest and inviting ocean are an irresistible combination. Those that make the journey over Takaka Hill to Golden Bay will find a hidden land of natural beauty from coastline to mountain. Dutch explorer Abel Tasman originally named this area Murderer's Bay in 1642 after several members of his crew were killed by local Maori. Captain James Cook, visiting in 1769, thankfully renamed it Golden Bay.

1 Marahau

This is a small settlement in a quiet valley right beside the Abel Tasman National Park. Services for visitors consist of a small shop, several cafés, kayak operators and some accommodation. From Marahau several companies operate scenic launch cruises and jet-boat water taxis around the Abel Tasman coastline. These operate on a daily scheduled basis, visiting all the beaches and accommodation.

2 Sea kayaking

Sea kayaking is the best way to observe the granite and limestone cliffs of the Abel Tasman coastline. You'll also see a variety of seabirds and perhaps a New Zealand fur seal. Join a guided trip, or hire a kayak if experienced.

3 Hiking the Abel Tasman Coast Track

The very accessible and popular Coastal Track meanders around the coastline, sometimes 150 m above sea level, sometimes right beside the beach. Day walks can be combined with water taxis and kayaks to enhance the experience. The whole 51-km track is usually walked in 3–4 days.

4 Awaroa Lodge and Restaurant

Awaroa Lodge offers first-class accommodation, a restaurant and eco-activities on a patch of private land surrounded by the Abel Tasman National Park. You can stay for days, or take a day-trip there by water taxi or light aircraft. Walk the tracks, kayak the coast, and enjoy a delicious lunch.

5 Sailing

There are two ways to sail around the Abel Tasman coastline from Marahau: join a skippered sailing trip, or experienced yachties can hire a yacht 'bareboat' for independent exploring.

6 Tonga Island Marine Reserve

This marine reserve protects the waters between Awaroa Head and Bark Bay from

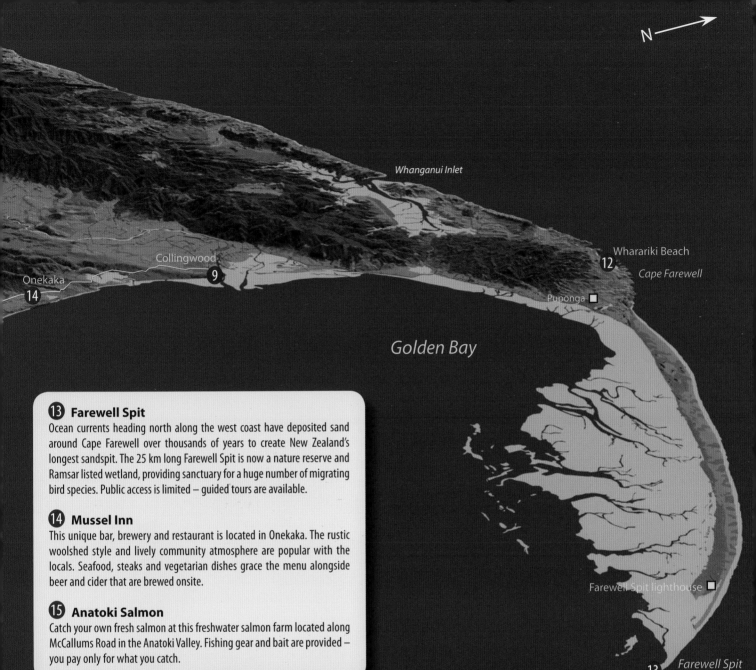

Whanganui Inlet

Collingwood

Onekaka

9

14

Wharariki Beach

12

Cape Farewell

Puponga ■

Golden Bay

13 Farewell Spit
Ocean currents heading north along the west coast have deposited sand around Cape Farewell over thousands of years to create New Zealand's longest sandspit. The 25 km long Farewell Spit is now a nature reserve and Ramsar listed wetland, providing sanctuary for a huge number of migrating bird species. Public access is limited – guided tours are available.

14 Mussel Inn
This unique bar, brewery and restaurant is located in Onekaka. The rustic woolshed style and lively community atmosphere are popular with the locals. Seafood, steaks and vegetarian dishes grace the menu alongside beer and cider that are brewed onsite.

15 Anatoki Salmon
Catch your own fresh salmon at this freshwater salmon farm located along McCallums Road in the Anatoki Valley. Fishing gear and bait are provided – you pay only for what you catch.

Farewell Spit lighthouse ■

13 *Farewell Spit*

---

fishing of any kind. Within the reserve is a small seal colony, mainly on Tonga Island, that can be observed during kayaking and scenic launch trips.

7 Harwoods Hole
Eons of erosion by water trickling through limestone rock has created Harwoods Hole, New Zealand's largest sinkhole. Located near the top of Takaka Hill, only experienced well-equipped cavers should explore the hole. For walkers, the track from the carpark to the hole is flat and easy. A 2 minute diversion leads up to a spectacular view towards the Takaka Valley.

8 Takaka
This is the largest town in Golden Bay offering everything you need for exploring the area – supermarket, DOC office, fuel and vibrant cafés (try the Wholemeal Café) for those who can't do without coffee.

9 Collingwood
The second largest town in Golden Bay has a couple of shops (with, most importantly, ice-cream) a museum, and an excellent little café. From here, several operators start bird-watching and nature day-trips to Farewell Spit Nature Reserve.

10 Pupu Springs
Golden Bay is well known for its labyrinth of caves, underground streams, sinkholes and springs. The most famous spring is Te Waikoropupu (Pupu) where water from the Takaka River emerges after flowing and filtering through the underlying gravel. Turn off down Pupu Valley Road, 9 km north of Takaka.

11 Heaphy Track
Inland from Collingwood is the northern entrance to the Heaphy Track. This Great Walk is the author's favourite, with an ever-changing variety of terrain as you hike across to the ruggedly beautiful west coast. Allow 4–5 days for the 82 km trip. Shuttle and light aircraft operators can transport you to and from both ends of the track.

12 Wharariki Beach
Walkers with average fitness can follow the 20-minute marked track across farmland and over large sand dunes to an impressively beautiful stretch of coastline on the west coast. Take a bottle of water and a sunhat.

ST ARNAUD & LAKE ROTOITI

Back in the mid-1800s Julius von Haast (of Haast Pass fame) predicted Lake Rotoiti would become a favourite destination for nature-lovers. He had good reason, given its incredibly beautiful alpine setting. However, as yet the small village of St Arnaud on the lake's northern shore has not quite taken off. This is probably due to its location slightly off the main travelling routes, which makes it all the more enjoyable for those that do venture inland.

Lake Rotoiti is the smaller, yet more popular, of the two lakes that form the heart of Nelson Lakes National Park. At St Arnaud village you can find accommodation, fuel, food and a café.

❶ DOC Office
The DOC office on View Road has information on all the local tracks as well as an interesting display explaining the Rotoiti Nature Recovery Project and the pest species in the area.

❷ Rotoiti Nature Recovery Project
This project protects over 800 ha of beech forest on the eastern side of the lake from introduced pests (deer, stoats, possums etc.) using a network of traps and other measures. As a result prolific birdlife can be seen and heard, including fantails, tui, robins and kaka. Wake up early to hear the dawn chorus.

❸ Bellbird, Honeydew and Loop Tracks
These three tracks are all loops, taking you into the Rotoiti Nature Recovery Project, starting from the carpark at the eastern end of Kerr Bay. The Bellbird Track is a flat and easy 10 minutes. The Honeydew Track has a short, gentle uphill section during its 35 minute loop. The Loop Track takes you even further, getting a lot steeper during its 90 minute duration and returning via the St Arnaud Range track.

❹ Lake Rotoiti Circuit and Whisky Falls
A circuit of the lake takes around 7–9 hours walking. The Lakehead Track follows the eastern shore of the lake to Lakehead Hut. From here cross Travers River (there is a swing-bridge 1.5 hours away if the river is in flood) to Coldwater Hut then follow the Lakeside Track back along the western side of the lake. You will pass the 40-metre-high Whisky Falls before joining Mt Robert Road to West Bay. For a walk to Whisky Falls from Mt Robert Road allow 2.5 hours each way.

❺ St Arnaud Range Track to the Ridgeline
This track will get your legs aching and heart pumping. From the carpark at the eastern end of Kerr Bay the track heads uphill and gets nice and steep, zigzagging as it climbs through progressive stages of vegetation. The large beech trees give way to tussock, small shrubs and alpine herbs. Just above the bushline is Parachute Rock (named after a parachute-shaped gravel fan), which has fine enough views if you decide the ridgeline is unnecessary. Allow 5 hours for the return trip to the ridgeline.

❻ Brunner Peninsula Nature Walk
The Brunner Peninsula juts into the lake, separating Kerr Bay from West Bay. The Nature Walk starts at the western end of Kerr Bay beach and follows the peninsula around to West Bay. You can return to Kerr Bay or the village by turning uphill and meeting Baxter or Cotterell streets (allow 90 minutes). Other options are to continue around the nature walk and connect with a track up to Rotoiti Lodge or go on to Mt Robert Road and take the Moraine Walk back to town.

❼ Mt Robert Circuit
From the end of Mt Robert Road two tracks climb Mt Robert to meet at the ridgeline, forming a circuit track. Allow 5 hours for the round trip. The Pinchgut Track zigzags steeply up the fire-affected open face of Mt Robert. Paddys Track goes around the face of the mountain then uphill. There are two shelters and a hut along the track.

❽ Lake Angelus
No guide book would be complete without mentioning this 2–3 day hiking trip that offers 360-degree views during a ridgeline walk to a small, chilly lake in a basin created by glacial action. You will encounter native forest, tussock, herb-fields and birdlife. There are three ways to reach the small hut at Lake Angelus: Mt Robert Ridge Track (7–8 hours); Speargrass Track (6–8 hours); or the longest option – around Lake Rotoiti and up the Cascade Track (8–9 hours). Choose any two of these and you have a circuit, but good fitness is required. Check the weather, book ahead, and carry full gear as conditions can deteriorate quickly even in summer.

NELSON LAKES NATIONAL PARK

Lake Angelus 8

8

Travers River

Lakehead Hut

Coldwater Hut

Mt Robert

Paddys Track

7

7

Whisky Falls 4

Pinchgut Track

4

Speargrass Track

Lake Rotoiti Circuit

4

Lake Rotoiti

3 Loop Track

Honeydew Track

Brunner Peninsula

6

3

Kerr Bay

West Bay

3 Bellbird Walk

3 picnic area

St Arnaud

DOC office 1

SH63 to MURCHISON

LEWIS PASS

Lewis Pass is the least travelled of the three main passes that cross the Southern Alps. This is probably due to the delights of the Lewis Pass highway and Nelson region being under-appreciated by most travellers. This journey is notable for its scenic variety and the Maruia Hot Springs. Whether you travel the highway in one day or several, you will enjoy the wonderfully untouched beech forest and alpine views, and variety of quiet walking tracks. This highway is a true pleasure to drive.

❶ Springs Junction

Located at the junction of SH 7 and SH 65, this small settlement is mainly a refreshment stop for travellers between Nelson, Christchurch and the West Coast. A café, petrol station and motels are the main services provided.

❷ Lake Daniells Track

Four km east of Springs Junction at the Marble Hill picnic and camping area you will find the track to Lake Daniells. A footbridge crosses over the narrow 'Sluice Box', where the Maruia River has sliced through the hard granite, then the relatively easy track ambles gently uphill through beautiful native beech forest. The moss- and fern-covered forest eventually reveals Lake Daniells. The small jetty makes a good picnic spot, or you can shelter at the hut in poor weather. Allow 2 hours each way. If you have an extra 2 hours carry on around the lake on the less-travelled section to Thompsons Flat Hut (1 hour each way).

❸ Waterfall Nature Walk

This short 20-minute return walk is located on the south side of the highway, about 8 km from Springs Junction or Lewis Pass. The track leads up the side of a small stream, becoming quite narrow as it reaches the waterfall.

❹ Maruia Springs Thermal Resort

The thermal waters of these natural hot springs have been enjoyed by visitors since 1904. Located beside the Maruia River on the western side of the Lewis Pass, it is remote and quiet compared to the hot springs at Hanmer. Bathe in the outdoor hot pools with a view of the river, native forest and mountain-tops, or hire a private spa complete with shower and changing room. Other facilities at the resort include massage, ensuite accommodation, restaurant, café and bar. Note: defend yourselves from the very attentive sandflies – they attack any un-submerged body parts.

❺ Lewis Pass Loop Track and Lookout

At the very highest point of the Pass is a short, unformed road to a small parking area. From here the track starts a steep, forested ascent to a lookout with extensive views of the Freyberg Range and Lewis Pass Scenic Reserve. Return to the carpark via the loop track or continue upwards to the Lewis Pass Tops. Allow 45–60 minutes for the return loop track.

❻ Tarn Nature Walk

On the eastern side of Lewis Pass, 200 metres below the summit, is a parking area for the Tarn Nature Walk. This is an enjoyable 20-minute loop track around an alpine area of tarns and wetland vegetation. To extend your exercise, follow the track as it descends into Cannibal Gorge. This is also the northern end of the 5-day St James Walkway.

❼ St James Walkway

The term 'walkway' is perhaps a little tame for this 5-day track. Although suitable for moderately fit and experienced people, its location in an alpine area means care should be taken with preparation and appropriate gear as the weather can change very quickly. After ticking those boxes, set off and enjoy the variety of mountain views, native forest and birdlife, wetlands and streams, and a little high-country farmland for good measure. Stay in huts or pitch your tent. Public transport can get you there and back, and a secure parking and drop-off service is also available to or from both ends of the track.

❽ Sylvia Flats Picnic Area and Hot Spring

One km north of the Boyle River bridge, on the left hand side driving north, you will find the Sylvia Flats Picnic Area. Three minutes walk up the riverside track will take you to a completely undeveloped, natural hot spring that emerges right on the river's edge. If the pools have not been recently flooded by the river, and if previous visitors have maintained the side-walls, then settle in for a muscle-relaxing soak. Don't forget the sandfly repellent.

SPENSER RANGE

Waiau River

St James Walkway

7

Henry River

Cannibal Gorge

FREYBERG RANGE

OPERA RANGE

5

Lewis Pass
Loop Track

6

Lewis Pass
Tarn Nature Walk

Maruia Springs
Thermal Resort **4**

LIBRETTO RANGE

Boyle River

St James Walkway

Lewis River

Nina River

Sylvia Flats **8**

Boyle River

SH7 to CHRISTCHURCH

N

KARAMEA TO WESTPORT

The West Coast of the South Island has a wild-west feel to it. Some would say this is due to the gruff, no-nonsense, staunchly independent nature of the 'Coasters'. That may have been true in the past (they were the staunchest of striking miners in the early 1900s) but today they are a proud and friendly people, encouraging visitors to come and experience the natural wonders and history of a distinctly different part of New Zealand, 90% of which is protected within national parks and DOC land.

The word 'wild' is still a very relevant word for the West Coast, but today it applies to the landscape. Within the space of a few kilometres you can travel from storm-tossed coastline, through subtropical rainforest and glacier-carved valleys to the jagged peaks of snow-topped mountains.

The most remote parts of the West Coast accessible by road are Karamea and Jackson Bay (see the South Westland section). Karamea, 1.5 hours drive north of Westport, is a small rural settlement with its own micro-climate and unique natural landscapes. Westport is the main town at this end of the coast and a great base for exploring the area.

❶ Heaphy Track

The Heaphy Track was named after Charles Heaphy who explored the coastal part of the track north of Kohaihai in 1846. At 82 km long, it is New Zealand's longest Great Walk, traversing Kahurangi National Park from the West Coast to Golden Bay. The complete track is normally walked in 4–6 days but the first section, from the mouth of the Kohaihai River, offers a great day-walk opportunity.

❷ The Last Resort

Rather than a last resort, this café bar in the isolated settlement of Karamea is the first destination for thirsty hikers coming off the Heaphy Track. The meals are hot and the drinks are cold (or hot). You can also rest your weary bones in the Last Resort's accommodation, including 2-bedroom cottages and backpacker rooms.

❸ Charming Creek Walkway

At Ngakawau, 35 km north of Westport, turn right to find this historic track, originally created for a railway by the Charming Creek Coal Company. The track is relatively flat and passes through a feast of natural features: massive boulders in the Ngakawau River, sheer cliffs, native forest and waterfalls, with railway tunnels and mining relics. Allow at least 3 hours one way for walking the 10.5 km. The other end of the track can also be reached by car from near Seddonville.

❹ Oparara Basin

About 9 km past Karamea turn right down an unsealed forestry track towards the Oparara Basin. Another 14 km of twisting, narrow road will reveal the first carpark for access to several limestone arches, and a second carpark for access to several caves. The tracks vary between 10–60 minutes each way. Inside the caves (take a torch) you will find limestone formations and fossils, cave spiders and other creepy insects. Guided tours are available.

❺ Tauranga Bay Seal Colony / Cape Foulwind Walkway

From the carpark at Tauranga Bay an easy 5-minute walk takes you to viewing points from where you can look down on a colony of New Zealand fur seals. The seals can reek a little if you get too close but they are not the reason for the name Cape Foulwind. Rather, Captain Cook named it for the difficult or 'foul' winds he experienced around the area. Continue along the track for sea views and other seal haul-out spots. You may even spot a blue penguin or the locally threatened sooty shearwater. Allow 1–1.5 hours each way for the complete Cape Foulwind Walkway.

❻ Bay House Café and Restaurant

This restaurant at the southern end of Tauranga Bay has a wonderful outlook over the sandy beach. Entertainment is provided by local surfers enjoying the often substantial waves. The meals are delicious, using fresh New Zealand produce and local seafood. Open from 10 am until late, 7 days (9 am on weekends).

❼ Helicopter Flights

The existence of Helicopter Charters Karamea opens up a whole raft of recreational opportunities in Kahurangi National Park. Options include a transfer to various points along the Heaphy Track (eg fly to Heaphy Hut and walk out) and other tracks, fishing trips, hunting trips and scenic flights along the coast.

❽ Charleston and the Nile River Valley

Roughly 30 km south of Westport you will find the historic village of Charleston. Having started and thrived as a gold-mining town, today it is a sleepy spot with one tavern and a sheltered little stony beach – a good picnic spot. Hidden away in the forested hills behind Charleston is the massive Nile River limestone cave system. Norwest Adventures take guided trips into the caves, ranging from walking trips for averagely fit people to full-on adventure caving with abseiling and tight squeezes. There are fantastic limestone formations and thousands of glow-worms.

❾ Buller Gorge

If your travels take you through the impressive Buller Gorge you won't regret it. The Buller is one of many powerful rivers carving their way through the beautiful West Coast landscape.

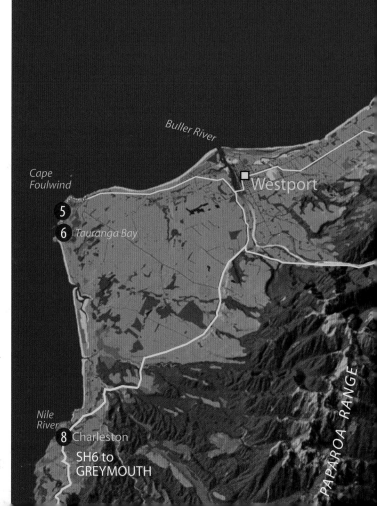

Heaphy Track

Heaphy River ■ Heaphy Hut

Scotts Beach
Kohaihai River ①

Oparara
Basin ④

KAHURANGI NATIONAL PARK

Karamea
Karamea River ② — ⑦
Last Resort

Little Wanganui River

Mokihinui River

■ Seddonville

Charming Creek
Walkway
③

■ Ngakawau

GLASGOW RANGE

SH6 to
NELSON
ST ARNAUD

■ Denniston

MT WILLIAM RANGE

Murchison ■

Buller River

■ Inangahua

SH65 to
LEWIS PASS

Buller Gorge

SH69 to
REEFTON

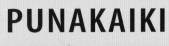

Ballroom Overhang

cave
5

Fox River Track

Inland Pack Track

SH6 to WESTPORT

Fox River

Kaipakati Point

Pahautane

← N

Meybille Bay

Irimahuwheri Bay

Perpendicular Point

Truman Track

3

Located halfway between Westport and Greymouth, the small settlement of Punakaiki is best known for the Pancake Rocks and Blowholes, the most outstanding feature of this precious limestone landscape. Take a closer look and you will find some wonderful walking tracks leading through lush native forest, alongside tannin-stained rivers, up isolated ravines and down to storm-tossed stony beaches. All this is part of Paparoa National Park, created in 1987 to protect the important granite mountains, limestone caves, river canyons, rainforest and wildlife.

❶ DOC Visitor Centre, Cafés and Crafts

Visitors to Punakaiki are well served by several busy little cafés just opposite the entrance to the Pancake Rocks track. You can also find a variety of creations by local artists, internet access, a public phone and the very informative Department of Conservation visitor centre. Evening meals are available 2 km further north at the Punakaiki Tavern or 1 km south at the Punakaiki Rocks Hotel.

❷ Pancake Rocks and Blowholes

Resembling huge stacks of pancakes, this intriguing headland has alternating layers of limestone and mudstone. Once uplifted by seismic action the rain, wind and seawater weathered the softer mudstone layers forming the pancake effect seen today. The crashing ocean waves have undermined parts of the headland creating several blowholes, which perform best within 2 hours of high tide while the wind blows onshore. Follow the well-formed track (suitable for wheelchairs to most features) through a massive flax forest and around the headland. Allow 20 minutes return and take care with children.

❸ Truman Track

Drive 3 km north of the DOC visitor centre to a small parking area. After 10–15 minutes walk along an easy track through lush subtropical forest, featuring rata trees and nikau palms, you will arrive at the coast overlooking a stony beach and rocky outcrops. At low tide it is safe to descend a short stairway to the beach. This is a delightful little beach with naturally carved cliffs and a small waterfall part-way along. It's a great place for a picnic, but swimming is discouraged.

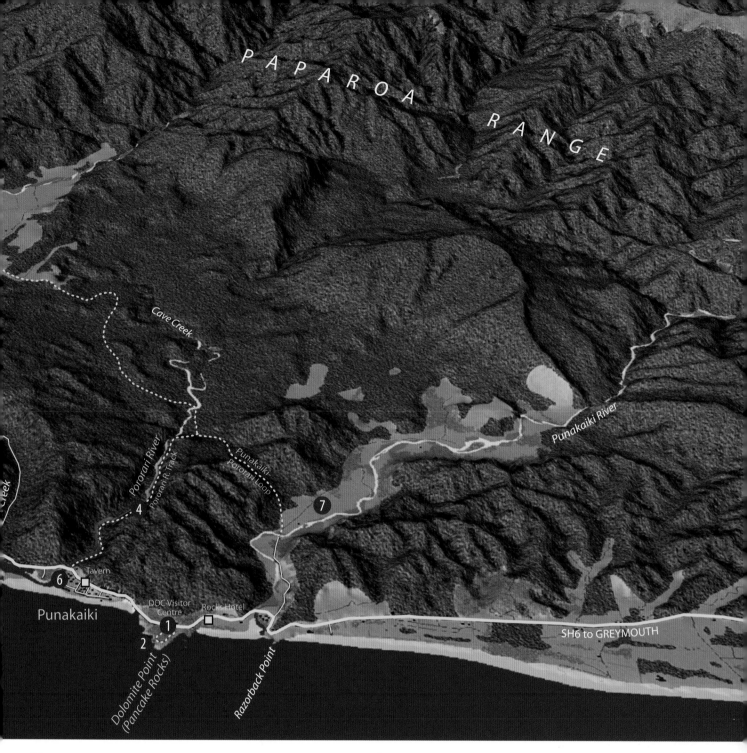

4 Pororari River Track

The Pororari River is 1 km north of the DOC visitor centre, just past the Punakaiki Tavern. From the parking area, walk under the bridge, through an impressive stand of nikau palm trees, and up the riverside track as far as the Inland Pack Track. The subtropical native forest fringes the riverbed which flows through an impressive limestone gorge. This easy but undulating track can be walked there and back (up to 1.5 hours each way) or as part of the Punakaiki–Pororari Loop walk (3.5 hours round trip). Check the track condition with DOC as it is subject to some erosion and repair at the time of writing.

5 Fox River Track and Cave

The Fox River meets the ocean 12 km north of Punakaiki. From the carpark walk along the northern side of the river for approximately an hour to where the main track requires a river crossing and continues upriver. If your objective is to visit the cave, stay on the northern bank track to the cave entrance. A torch or headlamp is required to explore this safe, 200-metre-long cave which has some interesting natural formations.

6 Punakaiki Canoes

An alternative way to explore the Pororari River is to paddle upstream in a canoe hired from the operator's base by the Pororari River bridge, 1 km north of the DOC visitor centre. Beginners can explore the lower reaches and lagoon, while more experienced people can head upstream through the limestone gorge. Get advice on the river conditions – you may need to get out of the canoe and walk some sections if they're shallow or swift, and it is best avoided when the river is in flood. Independent rentals and guided trips are available.

7 Punakaiki Horse Treks

Fans of horse riding will enjoy this non-mechanised way of exploring the natural attractions of the Punakaiki area. The guided horse treks wander through the river and native forest of the Punakaiki valley, then continue down to the coast and along the beach to a viewpoint of the Dolomite Point pancake rock formations. Treks are 2.5 hours long.

FRANZ JOSEF

MAIN DIVIDE SOUTHERN ALPS

Franz Josef Glacier

BAIRD RANGE

BURSTER RANGE

5

2

Sentinel Rock ▫

6

Lake
Wombat

Tatare Tunnels Walk **3**

1

Franz Josef
Hukawai Glacier Centre

4 **8**

Tatare Stream

Potters Creek

Waiho Loop (old terminal moraine)

SH6 to
WHATAROA
HOKITIKA

9 **Lake Mapourika**
Mapourika was created when the terminal moraine at the face of a glacier
collected water as the glacier retreated. A parking area and jetty provide a
great picnic spot. A local kayak company provides guided trips and kayaks for
solo hire – a great way to explore the rainforest edge of the lake.

Okarito   **7**

Aoraki/Mt Cook

Mt Tasman

RANGE

Alex Knob

SH6 to
FOX GLACIER

Docherty Creek

...iho River

N

Your South Island travels would be incomplete without exploring the South Westland area. The mountainous topography and lush subtropical rainforest is a wonderland for those that appreciate raw, undisturbed nature. The most powerful representations of nature are the glaciers that have created the landscape.

Of the hundred or so glaciers in the Westland region only the Franz Josef and Fox glaciers still flow down into the rainforest. Their unique situation results from a combination of a relatively fast descent through steep topography, and high annual rain and snowfall collected at the top of the glacier.

❶ DOC Visitor Centre

Make this your first stop when arriving in Franz Josef. Fascinating displays about the rugged geography, massive rainfall and natural processes of the area will awaken a sense of awe within you.

❷ Glacier Valley Walk & Sentinel Rock Walk

From the glacier carpark a well-formed track leads up the valley. The first sign points left to the Sentinel Rock walk, an easy uphill track to a glacier viewpoint (10 minutes each way). The main Glacier Valley track continues up the riverbed to the face of the glacier (40 minutes each way) and may require a little hop-step-jump across small streams. Obey all the warning signs and barriers – don't get too close to the glacier.

❸ Tatare Tunnels Walk

This track starts from the end of Cowan Street. Take a torch and raincoat for the tunnel. The track begins with a gentle 20-minute uphill section, then gets steeper up to the tunnels and tailrace, where you will find beautiful native bush, views of Tatare Gorge, and glow-worms at night. Allow 1.5 hours return.

❹ Hukawai Glacier Centre

This attraction, opened in February 2007, is an indoor, all-weather version of Franz Josef's glacier and rainforest environment. Explore ice-caves and native flora with audio-visual and 3D technology to interpret this dynamic habitat – great for a rainy day. They also have an indoor ice-climbing wall and café.

❺ Guided Glacier Hiking

Join a local guiding company for a safe and educational hike up and onto the glacier. 'Heli-hikes' combine a short helicopter ride up to the centre of the glacier to see extra ice formations and caves. Strong boots with crampons, hiking sticks, jackets and other warm clothing are usually provided.

❻ Lake Wombat and Alex Knob Track

Lush native forest surrounds the track as it climbs gently from the glacier access road to the small Lake Wombat (allow 1.5 hours return). The track to Alex Knob leads off to the left, just before the lake, and has some steep sections. Along the way you will pass through several stages of alpine vegetation and reach viewpoints of the glacier and Alps. If planning to go all the way to Alex Knob (8 hours return), start early to beat the clouds that commonly obscure views in the afternoon.

❼ Okarito

Okarito is 15 km north of Franz Josef and has three fascinating features: the unmodified wetland lagoon which is home to the white heron and other bird and plant life; the unique kiwi subspecies called the Okarito brown kiwi; and the fascinating history of the small community. Bird-watching, kiwi-spotting and kayak nature tours are available, starting from Whataroa or Okarito. There are also several walking tracks in this area.

❽ Scenic Flights

The most spectacular views are always achieved from on high, which is why there are several scenic flight operators located in this dramatic alpine area. Fixed-wing and helicopter flights carry you up and around the mountains, across the Main Divide and back. Ski-planes and helicopters can land on the glaciers and other remote places for stunning views of the Southern Alps in all directions.

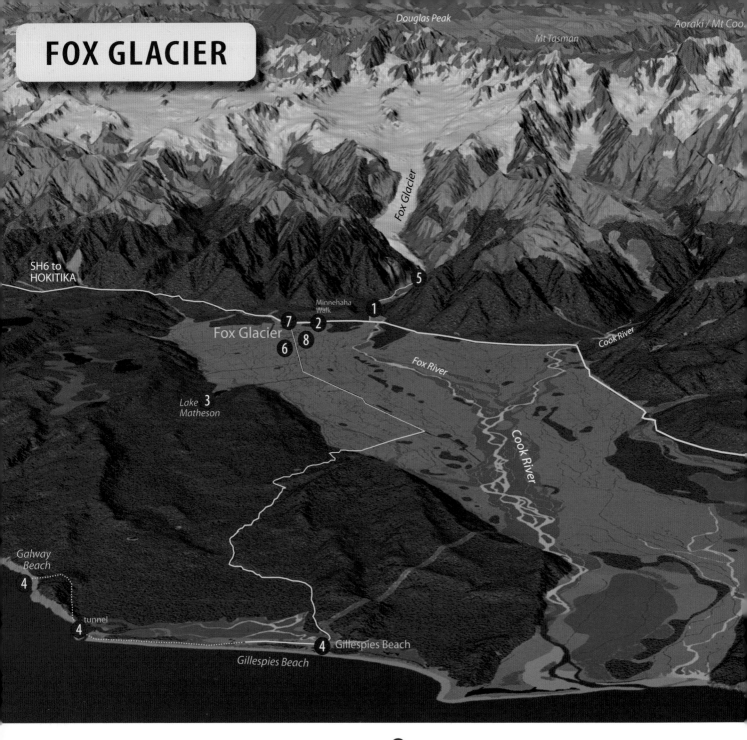

FOX GLACIER

Douglas Peak

Mt Tasman

Aoraki / Mt Coo...

Fox Glacier

SH6 to
HOKITIKA

Minnehaha
Walk

Fox Glacier

Cook River

Fox River

Cook River

Lake
Matheson

Galway
Beach

tunnel

Gillespies Beach

Gillespies Beach

The village at Fox is smaller than Franz Josef but the natural attractions are just as spectacular. The glacier was named after Sir William Fox, an early New Zealand Prime Minister. Like Franz Josef, Fox Glacier is roughly 12 km long, reaching from the jagged mountain tops down into rainforest only 300 metres above sea level.

Both glaciers are contained within Westland/Tai Poutini National Park, part of the South West New Zealand World Heritage Area. Stretching from the coast to the mountain tops, this wilderness has a wide diversity of natural landscapes and habitat types, and is home to some unique species. The rugged, isolated nature of the landscape resisted early exploitation by humans and so provides wonderful recreational experiences via a network of tracks and local operators.

❶ Glacier Valley Walk

Roughly 6 km from Fox village you will find the valley carpark. From here an easy track follows the riverbed to the face of the glacier. Spot the large blocks of 'dead' ice buried under rock beside the track. A small stream may need to be negotiated. Allow 30 minutes each direction and respect the signs and barriers – they are there for your safety. Driving to the carpark is recommended, rather than walking, to avoid the dusty roadway.

❷ Minnehaha Walk and Glow-worm Grotto

At the southern edge of town you will find the entrance to the Glow-worm Grotto. This is a short 3-minute nocturnal walk to view the luminescent larval stage of the fascinating *Arachnocampa luminosa* – a tiny flying gnat. The Minnehaha walk is 150 metres along the road past the Grotto. This easy 15-minute track wanders through a lush fern- and moss-covered forest beside a small stream.

❸ Lake Matheson

Perhaps the most photographed little lake in New Zealand, Lake Matheson is surrounded by native forest through which a well-formed, gentle track meanders. From the far end of the lake Mt Tasman and Aoraki/Mt Cook can be seen on a clear day. The lake's famous reflections are best observed very early in the morning, though the secret is out and you will see lots of people there from daybreak – but anytime is a good time. Allow 1.5 hours for the loop track.

❹ Gillespies Beach, Miners Tunnel and Galway Beach

Gillespies Beach is reached via 20 km of twisting road, half of which is unsealed, through native forest. Several tracks lead to the historic remains of a gold-mining

Mt Sefton

Copland Track

9

Copland Track

Karangarua River

SH6 to HAAST
WANAKA

N

settlement and up to a tunnel built so that travellers could avoid the difficulties of Gillespies Point (80 minutes return). A side track just before the tunnel leads to the isolated Galway Beach where seals commonly haul out to rest (3.5 hours return).

⑤ Guided Glacier Hiking
A local operator provides guided trips onto the glacier, either on foot or by helicopter. Check with the operator to make sure your fitness and agility match the difficulty of the access track. Strong boots with crampons, hiking sticks, jackets and other warm clothing can be provided, but take your own water and snacks.

⑥ Scenic Flights
Several scenic flight operators can fly you around this mountainous area, including Aoraki/Mt Cook and Mt Tasman, with the spectacular option of landing on one of the huge névés, the area at the top of the glacier where snowfall collects.

⑦ Mountain Bike Hire
A good way to explore the area. Hire a bike and helmet for leg-powered transport to Lake Matheson (flat riding), the glacier valley carpark (also flat), and up the

old glacier access road on the south side of Fox River to the start of the Chalet Lookout track (a more energetic climb). Note that none of the forest walking tracks are suitable for mountain bikes.

⑧ Whitebait
Whitebait (inanga) are a delicacy on the West Coast. These tiny native fish run the rivers between August and November and are caught, cooked and traditionally served in an egg or pikelet-style batter with a wedge of lemon. Many restaurants, pubs, and cafés serve their own particular recipe and all are delicious. A must-try during any West Coast visit.

⑨ Copland Track to the Welcome Flat Hot Pools
The Copland valley is located roughly 30 km south of Fox village. The track that follows the valley floor leads to the Welcome Flat natural hot pools and DOC hut, which are very popular. From the road end to the pools is 17 km (allow at least 7 hours one way) so this is usually done as an overnight excursion for reasonably fit hikers. Purchase hut tickets, and check weather and track conditions at the nearest DOC office.

SOUTH WESTLAND & HAAST PASS

As you drive towards Haast Pass, from the north or south, you encounter such a continuous change in natural features that this is considered to be New Zealand's most stunning one-day journey. Haast Pass is located within Mount Aspiring National Park, which is itself part of Te Wahipounamu/South West New Zealand World Heritage area. Be warned, South Westland is the ancestral homeland for the thirsty native sandfly, so be sure to take steps to protect your blood supply.

❶ Bruce Bay
A small settlement remains at Bruce Bay after gold fever came and went. Take a walk along the beach and look for dolphins cruising by.

❷ South Westland Salmon Farm
In the midst of the South Westland wilderness, this seems an unusual place to find a café serving fresh salmon, prepared in a dozen delicious ways. Located 68 km south of Fox Glacier, or 55 km north of Haast, by the Paringa River.

❸ Monro Beach
Monro Beach is a flat 25–30 minute walk (each way) from the carpark on the northern side of Moeraki River. Fiordland crested penguins are frequently seen along this beach between July and December.

❹ Knights Point Lookout
The road climbs to this high point looking west over the Tasman Sea. Knights Point was the final section of SH 6 to be completed in 1965, finally linking Central Otago and Haast with the rest of the West Coast. Knight was the dog owned by the road surveyor!

❺ Ship Creek and Waita Beach Walks
This is central HQ for the carnivorous sandfly, but stop to view the ocean waves sweeping the stony coastline – a beautiful place. Short walks from here include the 20-minute Kahikatea Swamp Forest walk that follows Ship Creek into a swampy patch of kahikatea. Boardwalks make it flat and easy. Another track takes you south alongside the beach and through wind-beaten coastal forest to Dune Lake, a small lake created behind permanent dunes. Allow 30 minutes for the round trip, perhaps returning via the beach.

❻ Haast Township
To illustrate the past isolation of this small township, consider that the road between Haast and Fox Glacier was only completed in 1965. Today the town is somewhat scattered but has a very interesting DOC visitor centre. The few services here include a tiny supermarket, two petrol stations, a small café and several accommodation options. Two jet-boat companies operate here on either the Haast or Waiototo rivers. The one-way bridge just north of the town is one of New Zealand's longest bridges at 737 metres.

❼ Jackson Bay
If you have the time, explore to the end of the road at remote Jackson Bay, a small fishing settlement. Big plans were made for this area but the early settlers were unsuccessful, beaten by the harsh climate and isolation. The graves of early settlers can still be found at the Arawhata Pioneer Cemetery (10 km back from Jackson Bay). The main attraction at Jackson Bay has to be The Craypot, a restored pie-cart converted to cook fresh fish and chips – basic but tasty. Open daily between November and April but check with the DOC visitor centre in Haast to be sure.

❽ Makarora
If you are heading north over Haast Pass this small settlement is the last chance to get food and fuel. A restaurant/café is open from 8 am until late. Accommodation is also available, from tent sites and backpackers to ensuite cabins. The real attractions here are the activities: scenic flights, jet-boat rides, hiking and fishing.

Landsborough River

Mt Brewster

Pleasant Flat

Gates
of Haast

9

Fantail Falls

9

Thunder Creek Falls

Haast Pass

Roaring Billy Falls   9

Blue Pools   9

Cameron Creek
Cameron Flat

Makarora River

Makarora

8

SH6 to
WANAKA

Wilkin River

MOUNT ASPIRING NATIONAL PARK

9 Lookouts, Walks and Waterfalls

The Haast Highway has a number of lookouts, beautiful walks and impressive waterfalls easily accessed from the highway and all worthy of a visit. Most are well signposted and give information on walking times. They include Roaring Billy Falls, Pleasant Flat Picnic Area, Thunder Creek Falls, Fantail Falls, the Blue Pools, and Cameron Creek. Each has its own charm and captures the beauty of this varied, moss-laden beech forest, and the mighty Haast and Makarora rivers. Even when it's raining, the bush can be relatively sheltered, so don a raincoat and enjoy the fresh air, sights and smells of this magnificent area.

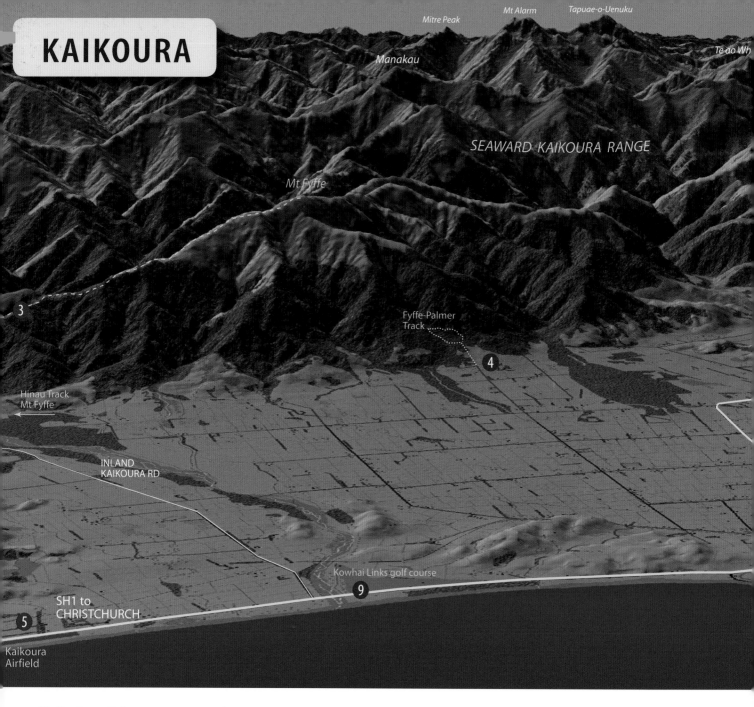

KAIKOURA

Mt Alarm
Tapuae-o-Uenuku
Mitre Peak
Manakau
Te ao Wh

SEAWARD KAIKOURA RANGE

Mt Fyffe

3

Fyffe-Palmer
Track
4

Hinau Track
Mt Fyffe

INLAND
KAIKOURA RD

Kowhai Links golf course
9

SH1 to
CHRISTCHURCH
5

Kaikoura
Airfield

The Maori name Kaikoura means 'to eat crayfish' (lobster) and reveals one reason why Maori settlers first made this small peninsula their home. Crayfish may be the local delicacy but they are only one of many different marine species that make Kaikoura a magnet for wildlife watchers and seafood-lovers. Favourable ocean currents bring krill and other marine food along the very deep Hikurangi Trench, creating a perfect feeding ground for various whale, dolphin, seal, fish and bird species.

Kaikoura is a small town with a little over 3000 people, mostly situated on the northern side of the peninsula that bears the same name. Look east towards the blue Pacific Ocean, and west to the massive Seaward Kaikoura mountain range. This is a beautiful place, which is perhaps the reason for there being few office jobs in town – who could spend all their days inside when living here?

❶ Kaikoura Peninsula Seal Colony and Walkway

Drive along the Esplanade through town on the northern side of the peninsula, and continue to the carpark at the end where you can often observe New Zealand fur seals resting on the shore – but stay at least 20 metres away for safety. The walkway first climbs for 5 minutes to the top of the limestone headland then continues around the cliff-top and through farmland for 1 hour to the southern side of the peninsula. Above Whalers Bay you can walk down a path to the rocky

beach and choose to return to the carpark at sea-level, but only while the tide is out (allow 45 minutes to return this way).

❷ Ohau Point Seal Colony

A few steps lead down to a viewing platform from where you can view a colony of New Zealand fur seals resting on the rocks below. The young pups can be seen playing in the rock pools during their first few months of life. Indicate your intention to stop quite early – this is a busy piece of the highway.

❸ Hinau Track and Mt Fyffe

From the Mt Fyffe carpark at the end of Postmans Road you can explore the Hinau Track, a reasonably flat walk around a loop track through hinau, mahoe and broadleaf forest (allow 45 minutes). Also from the Mt Fyffe carpark, a 4WD track climbs up and up to Mt Fyffe Hut (5 hours return) then beyond to the top of the mountain (8 hours return). Views from the top include the Kaikoura area and on a clear day may extend south to Banks Peninsula near Christchurch.

❹ Fyffe–Palmer Track

A reserve by the same name can be found at the end of Mt Fyffe Road. The forest is regenerating but there is a great variety of native species, a nice picnic area and

SH1 to BLENHEIM

2 *Ohau Point*

Hapuku River

Kaikoura

5
6 **7**
8

The Esplanade

1 seal colony

South Bay

Kaikoura Peninsula

Whalers Bay

N

great views stretching away to the horizon. It's a little steep in places, so allow up to 2 hours for the whole loop track.

5 **Whale Watching Cruises and Flights**

There are several options for viewing whales offshore. Whale Watch Kaikoura operates 3.5-hour tours (including 2.5 hours on the water) during which dolphins, seals and albatross may also be seen. Wings Over Whales (based at Kaikoura airport 7 minutes south of the town) operates 30-minute fixed-wing flights that may also include dolphin sightings and a scenic flight over the Kaikoura Peninsula. Kaikoura Helicopters offer 30- or 40-minute flights and longer options that can include landings on the Kaikoura mountains.

6 **Dolphin Encounter – Watching or Swimming with Dolphins**

This is a very popular way of observing and interacting with wild Dusky dolphins in a completely natural setting. During a 3-hour cruise you have the option of simply watching the dolphins' acrobatic antics from the comfort of the boat, or you can pull on a wetsuit, flippers and snorkel for a dip in the ocean. The wetsuits are very buoyant but water-confidence is an asset. Booking well ahead is advised.

7 **Pelagic Bird-watching Cruises**

You don't need to be a regular birdwatcher to enjoy an Ocean Wings bird-watching cruise. Trips start from their base along the Esplanade. The 2.5–3-hour cruises explore several sites frequented by albatross, terns, shags, gulls, petrels and more. The crew onboard will identify the birds and describe their migratory range and other characteristics.

8 **Fishing, Diving and Snorkelling Trips**

There's a reason all the whales, dolphins and seabirds hang around – the ocean is full of life. Join a local launch operator for fishing, scuba diving and snorkelling trips, either to catch your dinner or simply to get close to the various species that make this underwater habitat their home. There are several operators that take land- or boat-based seal swimming trips. Most gear can be provided.

9 **Kowhai Links Golf Course**

Located on SH 1 only 5 minutes drive south of Kaikoura, this 18-hole course has the incredible Seaward Kaikoura Range as a backdrop. Clubs, trundlers and golf carts are available for hire from the clubhouse.

HANMER SPRINGS

The discovery of natural hot springs in the late 1800s put Hanmer on the map. Located in North Canterbury, the small town of Hanmer is 10 km off SH 7 between Christchurch and Murchison. The hot springs are the main attraction but together with a good variety of outdoor activities this town becomes very popular during the summer and especially during school holidays. Winter is also a great time to enjoy the thermal waters when a carpet of snow lends an extra dimension to the experience. The greater Hanmer area was originally a tussock-grassed landscape but since 1900 various State and private forestry projects have created large forests of exotic varieties. Many of these forests are open for walks, picnics and mountain biking.

❶ Visitor Information Centre
Located on the eastern side of the hot springs complex.

❷ Thermal Hot Springs
Located right in the centre of town, Hanmer Springs Thermal Pools and Spa has various open-air thermal pools, private pools, saunas and other watery options for all ages. You can combine a thermal soak with massage and beauty therapies, and even dine at the on-site restaurant. By booking in advance you can arrange a package that can include entry to the pools, accommodation, massage and other services. Opening times are 10 am–9 pm every day except Christmas Day.

❸ Mountain Biking
Forest tracks and 4WD roads of all description and difficulty are available to mountain bikers, including the Heritage Forest right beside the town (see below). Bring your own bikes and helmets, or hire them from local companies. Guided trips are also possible.

❹ Conical Hill Track
From the centre of town walk up Conical Hill Road to reach the track that zigzags to the summit of the hill. Cheaters can drive up the road to reach the start of the track. The surrounding exotic forest includes Lawson and Japanese cypress. There are great views over the Hanmer basin from the summit shelter. Allow 1 hour return.

❺ Hanmer Heritage Forest
On the eastern side of town is an area of exotic forest over 100 years old. Now protected with a covenant that represents its importance to the Hanmer community, this forest of more than 60 species is an interesting contrast to the native New Zealand forests. Walking and mountain biking tracks criss-cross the forest, and small interpretation panels identify the different species. Access is possible from various points along Jollies Pass Road and Scarborough Terrace.

❻ Molesworth Station
With over 180,000 ha (500,000 acres) of stunning high-country land, Molesworth Station is New Zealand's largest farm. Located north of Hanmer Springs, Molesworth is managed by DOC but is open to the public for recreational pursuits such as multi-day hiking, 4WD, mountain-bike, rafting and horse-trek adventures. Some trips take you from Hanmer right through to Blenheim. Access to parts of Molesworth is restricted at certain times of the year – contact the Hanmer i-Site information centre for more information.

❼ Hanmer Golf Course
On the western side of town this 18-hole championship course has mountains for a scenic backdrop. Clubs and motorised golf carts are available for hire.

❽ Thrillseekers Canyon Adventure Centre
The natural features of Hanmer lend themselves to many other adventures. Thrillseekers offer a huge variety: jet-boats, rafting, bungy-jumping, claybird shooting, quad biking and more. Their base is located by the bridge over the Waiau Gorge, on the way into Hanmer Springs.

Waiau River

SH7 to
LEWIS PASS
SPRINGS JUNCTION
MURCHISON

Awatere River

MOLESWORTH COUNTRY

Clarence River

6

4 *Conical Hill* 3

Hanmer
Thermal Spa

HANMER
HERITAGE
FOREST 5

2 1

Golf
Course 7

HANMER

BASIN

SH7A

Canyon Adventure
Centre 8

N

SH7 to
CHRISTCHURCH

CHRISTCHURCH CITY

First-time visitors to Christchurch will quickly notice two things: the city is as flat as a pancake; and colourful gardens and trees line every street. The city slogan may now be 'Fresh Each Day' but Christchurch will always be the 'Garden City' to me.

Christchurch is located on the edge of the Canterbury Plains, the alluvial bridge between the Southern Alps and the two extinct volcanic cones of Banks Peninsula. In the 1850s European settlers worked hard to tame the sparse vegetation and wetlands of the original flood plain to create a productive farming community. Today this city of roughly 360,000 people thrives on farming, tourism and technology.

As you explore the central city the historic stone buildings, mostly within the four avenues of Bealey, Deans, Moorhouse and Fitzgerald, will give you an insight into the English colonial heritage. Built largely from locally quarried stone, they represent a fine collection of New Zealand's early architectural legacy.

❶ Canterbury Museum
First opened in 1867, the Canterbury Museum houses attractive and educational displays of New Zealand's natural heritage, Maori and European history, Victorian fashion, Antarctic exploration and a variety of touring exhibitions. Open daily except Christmas Day between 9 am and 5 pm.

❷ Christchurch Art Gallery
Opened in 2003, this strikingly modern building houses many important public art collections, including prominent New Zealand artists. Open daily except Christmas Day from 10 am–5 pm with a late night on Wednesdays until 9 pm.

❸ Christchurch Arts Centre and Weekend Market
The Arts Centre occupies the neo-gothic stone buildings originally constructed for the University of Canterbury. The university outgrew the site and moved out, allowing art, craft, culture and theatre to move in. Every Saturday and Sunday between 10 am and 4 pm the courtyard becomes a marketplace selling fashion, arts and crafts. Buskers entertain the crowds while food stalls offer cuisine ranging from Greek to Cambodian.

❹ Cathedral Square and Anglican Cathedral
The city's Anglican Cathedral in Cathedral Square was consecrated in 1881, and is constructed mainly of stone with 17 stained glass windows. Due to several earthquakes the 63-metre spire has been finished in copper rather than stone. The public can explore the cathedral's interior and climb to a viewing deck in the spire. Open Monday–Saturday from 9 am–5 pm (Sunday from 7.30 am).

❺ Christ's College
This private school for boys was planned back in England before the Canterbury colony was even established. Lessons began in Lyttelton in 1850 before the school moved to the current site in 1852, making it New Zealand's oldest school. Around the quadrangle stand the school's chapel, dining room, library and boarding houses, most built from stone and all of great historic value. Tours of the school (1 hour, $5) are conducted between October and April, on Mondays, Wednesdays and Fridays at 10 am. During term, Wednesday's tour includes listening to the congregational practice in the chapel.

❻ Avon River Punting
Punting on the Avon River is a leisurely way to explore the central city and enjoy the oh-so English character of the city. The iconic, tree-lined Avon meanders its way through the Botanic Gardens and Hagley Park. Departing from the Antigua Boat Sheds, the well-balanced punting crew will propel you along, explaining the scenery, while ducks and swans swim along or rest under the willow trees. Take some food and drink – champagne flutes can be supplied. Bookings are recommended.

❼ Christchurch Tramway
Completing a 2.5-km loop of the central city area every 25 minutes, Christchurch's trams are a defiant blast from the past. Electric trams were an important part of the city's public transport system from 1905 until 1954 when they were banished in favour of buses. Purchase tickets from the drivers, listen to the commentary, and jump on and off at tram-stops along the route as often as you like (tickets are valid for 2 days, with combo-ticket options available). In the evening a restaurant car serves dinner as you travel – bookings are essential.

❽ Hagley Park and the Botanic Gardens
The founding fathers (and mothers?) of Christchurch had the foresight to set aside a huge swathe of land in the city centre to recreate the traditional garden setting of their British homeland. What started with an oak tree in 1863 has become the Botanic Gardens: 30 ha (74 acres) of grassy lawns, flowerbeds and towering exotic trees, with a few New Zealand natives as well. The Avon River meanders through the gardens with ducks and trout enjoying the inner-city sanctuary. Almost encircling the Botanic Gardens is Hagley Park, 161 ha (395 acres) of fields for sports as diverse as rugby, tennis, netball and golf.

Christchurch Interr

SH1 to
TIMARU
DUNEDIN

AVONHEAD

BUR

ILAM

RICCARTON

Deans Av

❽ H

Mc

SYDENH

SPREYDON

CANTERBURY PLAINS

Waimakariri River

I Airport

SH1 to
KAIKOURA
BLENHEIM

HAREWOOD

REDWOOD

PAPANUI

FENDALTON

ST ALBANS

MAIREHAU

Hagley Park

Bealey Avenue

Christ's College

Canterbury Museum
Arts Centre/Market
Christchurch Art Gallery

ark

5

Botanic Gardens

1

Antigua Boat Sheds

3   2   Tramway   7

6   Avon River

4

Avon River

e Avenue

Cathedral
Square

Fitzgerald Avenue

LINWOOD

Catholic Cathedral

BROMLEY

ST MARTINS

WOOLSTON

N

SH74 to
LYTTELTON

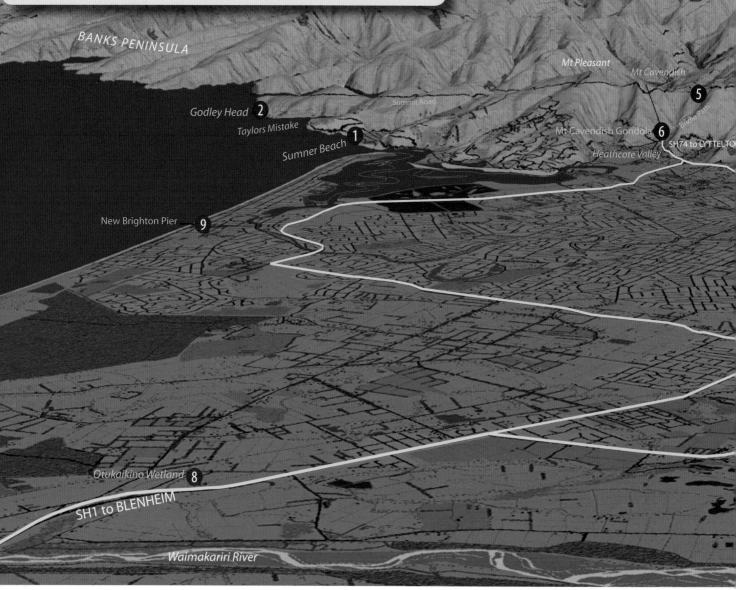

CHRISTCHURCH OUTSKIRTS

BANKS PENINSULA

Godley Head ②

Taylors Mistake

Sumner Beach ①

Mt Pleasant

Mt Cavendish

Summit Road

⑤

Mt Cavendish Gondola ⑥

SH74 to LYTTELTON

Heathcote Valley

New Brighton Pier ⑨

Otukaikino Wetland ⑧

SH1 to BLENHEIM

Waimakariri River

The South Island's largest city has historic and cultural attractions galore, lovely gardens and tree-lined parks. Often overlooked by guidebooks, there are still options for outdoor action around the city; including patches of original native bush; some historic sites; and walking tracks to high places.

① Sumner Beach

Sumner Beach is probably the city's favourite beach spot, great for a walk or dip in the ocean. There are cafés and an ice-cream shop just where they need to be – right beside the sand. A large outcrop of volcanic rock has caves (hence the name Cave Rock) that can be wandered through at low tide.

② Godley Head Recreation Area

Located around the eastern side of the Port Hills, Godley Head can be reached two different ways. Drive to Sumner then up Evans Pass Road to connect with Godley Head Road and a network of tracks. Or drive past Sumner and over the hill to the sandy beach at Taylors Mistake. From here a track climbs around the tussock-covered peninsula above high cliffs. Attractions include an historic WW II gun emplacement, observation posts and fantastic views out to sea. Tracks are for walkers and mountain bikers. Average fitness is required, and allow 1.5–2 hours one way between Taylors Mistake Beach and Godley Head.

③ Sign of the Takahe and Cracroft Reserve

The Sign of the Takahe is the most grand of four historic buildings created along the Summit Road as rest houses for people walking the Port Hills summit track. In front of the Takahe a 200-metre track through the Cracroft Reserve leads to a viewing point where features of the Canterbury Plains and the Southern Alps are engraved into a stainless steel table. With this diagram, on a clear day, it is possible to identify different mountains including Aoraki/Mt Cook, 200 km to the west.

④ Sign of the Kiwi and Sugarloaf Walks

Past the Takahe, further along the Summit Road, you will come to the Sign of the Kiwi. This is the second largest of the historic rest houses, carefully restored and now a quiet café. Across the road, opposite the café you will find the start of a series of tracks that form a circuit around Sugarloaf. You can't mistake Sugarloaf – it has a massive television transmitter at the top of it. Enjoy the mixture of native bush, tussock-land and 360-degree views of Christchurch city and Lyttelton Harbour.

⑤ Bridle Path

In 1851 a track was created from Lyttelton Harbour over the Port Hills and down into the Heathcote valley for newly arrived settlers to reach the growing settlement of Christchurch. From Bridle Path Road the track climbs to the crater rim where a memorial stands to honour the early pioneering women (allow 1 hour to the top, from either side). From the top you can see in every direction – down to

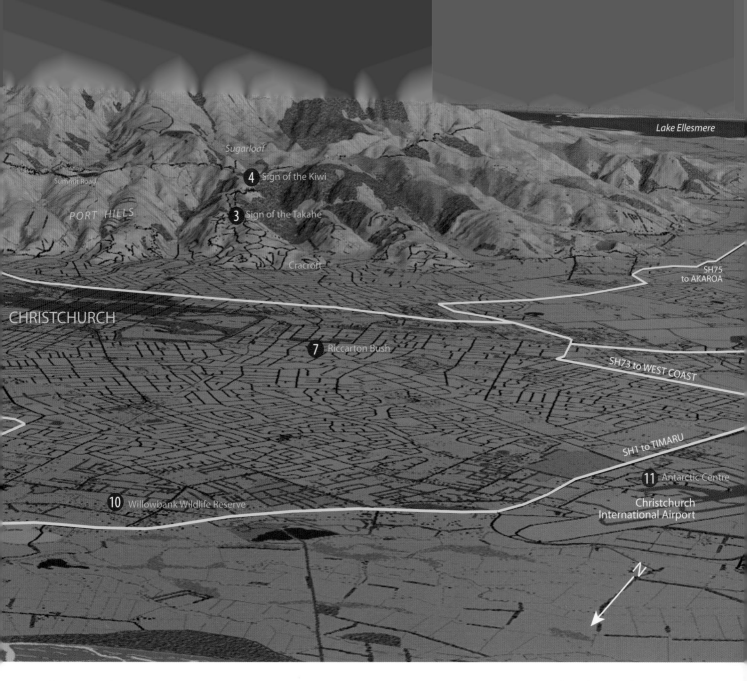

Lake Ellesmere

Sugarloaf

Summit Road

4 Sign of the Kiwi

PORT HILLS

3 Sign of the Takahe

Cracroft

CHRISTCHURCH

7 Riccarton Bush

SH75 to AKAROA

SH73 to WEST COAST

SH1 to TIMARU

11 Antarctic Centre

Christchurch International Airport

10 Willowbank Wildlife Reserve

Lyttelton, out over the city and across the Canterbury Plains to the Southern Alps. The track continues down to Lyttelton or you can walk along the crater rim to the Mt Cavendish Gondola (20 minutes) for a lazy way back down.

6 Mt Cavendish Gondola
Via the gondola you can do in 4 or 5 minutes what takes the Bridle Path walkers 90 minutes. The gondola rises to a restaurant and viewing platform 445 metres (1500 feet) above sea level. Also, unlike walking the Bridle Path, you can sip a latte while enjoying the sweeping views. Located on Bridle Path Road in the Heathcote Valley.

7 Riccarton Bush / Putaringamotu Public Reserve
Like a tiny island in the middle of an ocean, Riccarton Bush is a refreshing speck of nature surrounded by busy city life. And with the only remaining stand of original kahikatea forest in Christchurch, its natural heritage is immensely valuable. Of the 12-ha reserve, around half is native forest with the rest occupied by historic buildings, lawns and gardens. A pleasant nature walk and picnic spot.

8 Otukaikino Wetland Living Memorial
Otukaikino is a 13-ha wetland area on the northern outskirts of the city. A boardwalk loops around the wetland with information panels and seating areas. After decades of neglect the reserve is being restored and replanted as a 'living

memorial'. Information about the memorial and its cultural significance to Ngai Tahu people is explained at the wetland entrance.

9 New Brighton Pier
The original pier on this site led a troubled life between opening in 1894 until its demolition in 1964. The current pier opened to the public in 1997, and is 300 metres long and 7 metres above the high tide sea level.

10 Willowbank Wildlife Reserve
Willowbank is a well-designed nature reserve for learning about many of New Zealand's wildlife species, as well as environment and conservation issues. Wander through different open enclosures, including a kiwi-house, eel-pond, aviaries and farmyard. Several programmes are underway to protect and breed endangered species. Willowbank is open from 10 am every day. In the evening you can be guided through the outdoor kiwi enclosure, see the Ko Tane Maori cultural performance and have a buffet dinner.

11 Antarctic Centre
This facility is as close as you will get to the Great White Continent without a long sea journey. A series of walk-through exhibits recreate the snowscape and climate of the real thing. Slide around in the snow, experience an Antarctic storm and go for a ride in the Hagglund caterpillar vehicle.

Pigeon Bay

Lyttelton Harbour

☐ *Mt Herbert*

Hill **2**

Kaituna valley

Little River **1**

Okuti Valley Rese **8**

SH75 to CHRISTCHURCH

Lake Forsyth

Banks Peninsula was originally an island, created by two separate volcanoes exploding out of the Pacific Ocean between 8 and 11 million years ago. Over time, both volcanic craters eroded, allowing the sea to flood in and create natural harbours. Eroded material from the Southern Alps eventually joined this island to the mainland. Native forest has largely been replaced by farmland but there are a few scattered reserves and enticing bays and beaches.

Several different Maori tribes occupied the Peninsula over time until European whalers started to arrive in the early 1800s. A brave group of French and German migrants intended to establish a colony at Akaroa ('long harbour') but were stymied by the British who arrived only days before them, raising their flag and declaring British sovereignty over the whole South Island. The French settlers decided to stay anyway and established a slice of France that is still celebrated today.

❶ Little River
A long, winding road up a big hill is just ahead of you so stop here for ice-cream and other refreshments at the store and café. Attached to the café is a very nice gallery featuring sculpture, jewellery and paintings by local artists.

❷ The Hilltop Tavern and Lookout
The road between Christchurch and Akaroa climbs to the crater rim before descending into Akaroa Harbour. Just over the summit, turn right towards Akaroa and you will find the Hilltop Tavern. Stop here for a pint of beer or quick meal, and gain your first view of Akaroa Harbour stretching away to the south.

❸ Barrys Bay Cheese Factory
As you reach the bottom of the hill you arrive at Barrys Bay. Located here is a tiny cheese factory making delicious traditional cheeses from local milk supplies. Open daily all year round for sales of cheese and other local food products. Cheese-making can be viewed on alternate days between mid-September until mid-May.

❹ Cruise or Swim with Dolphins
Several operators cruise the length of the harbour, right out to the open ocean. Cruises start from the main Akaroa wharf, and along the way crew point out the various geological features, dolphins and other wildlife, and explain the history of the area. Dolphin-swimming is an option, with wetsuits provided.

❺ Akaroa Museum
This well-presented museum at 71 Rue Lavaud records and explains the history and culture of the Akaroa and wider Banks Peninsula communities. The historic Court House, Custom House, and Langlois Eleveneaux Cottage contain artefacts,

photographs, displays and audio-visual programmes explaining the stories of the local people, starting with the Maori and the whalers, and continuing to contemporary Akaroa.

6 Pohatu-Flea Bay Penguin Colony and Marine Reserve

Over the hill from Akaroa, on the south-east coast, you will find this small but delightful bay. Above the sandy beach a colony of white-flippered penguins is nurtured and protected by the dedicated landowners – join them for a guided introduction to the colony. Flea Bay and the cliffs, islands and caves of the open coastline are contained within a marine reserve. Kayaks and snorkelling gear are available for hire. The Akaroa-Pohatu road is steep, narrow and unsealed, recommended for 4WD vehicles only.

7 Isolated Bays and Beaches

For a slice of quiet, coastal farming life venture over the crater rim and drive down to one of the small eastern bays. Little Akaloa, Okains, Le Bons and Otanerito bays all have sandy beaches great for swimming. Okains Bay also has a small general store and special little museum about early Maori and European settlement. The road down to Otanerito Bay passes through the Hinewai Reserve which has several walking tracks.

8 Scenic Reserves

Scattered about the peninsula are tiny patches of native bush now protected as scenic reserves. The Okuti Valley Scenic Reserve is reached by turning right just before Little River and following Okuti Valley Road for 4 km. Mixed lowland forest is home to abundant native birdlife. Allow 20 minutes for the loop track. Otepatotu Scenic Reserve can be found along the Summit Road between Okains Bay and Le Bons Bay. Otepatotu translates as 'place of the fairies', named for the moss hanging from trees near the summit of Lavericks Peak. The 1-hour loop track takes you to a very scenic lookout before climbing up and through the forest, returning eventually to the picnic area. Other reserves include the Kaituna, Hay and Akaroa Head scenic reserves.

9 Banks Peninsula Track

This 35-km track explores the coastline, native forest, wildlife and farmland of 8 local families located around the south-eastern side of the peninsula. Moderately fit walkers can choose between the 2-day or 4-day options, staying in comfortable self-contained bunk accommodation. Walkers cover between 6 and 11 km each day. Transport to and from the track, kitchens, hot showers and pack cartage are available. Food and refreshments are available from two small shops along the way. Space is limited on this popular walk and must be pre-booked

ARTHUR'S PASS

Of the three main state highways that cross the Southern Alps, Arthur's Pass reaches the highest altitude. The highest point is actually at Porters Pass (946 metres), a good 65 km east of Arthur's Pass (924 metres).

Prior to the Europeans' arrival, Maori used this alpine route to reach the West Coast in search of greenstone (jade). In 1864 explorer Arthur Dudley Dobson discovered the route and his name became permanently attached to it when it was chosen to become the main coast-to-coast road. A memorial to Arthur Dobson stands at the summit of the pass.

The 4-hour journey from Christchurch to the West Coast is sublime. The flat farmland of the Canterbury Plains soon changes to river valleys, high mountains, alpine lakes and forest. Don't just drive it though, allow extra time to stop for the alpine views, bush walks and of course a picnic lunch. Another option is to travel on the Tranz Alpine train, which takes a slightly different route and involves a long tunnel under the actual pass. If you have the chance to spend a few days in the area, all standards of accommodation are available. The options for dining out however are limited.

❶ Kura Tawhiti Conservation Area (Castle Hill)
Located about 5 km west of Porters Pass, the naturally sculptured karst (limestone) rock formations of the Kura Tawhiti Conservation Area are culturally significant for the Ngai Tahu people of the South Island. Their traditions and stories relate back to ancestors who cultivated kumara (sweet potato) here and traversed the area in search of kakapo and other resources. A short 5-minute walk will take you across farmland to the limestone rocks. Please keep to the track and walk in the open space between the rocks to avoid damage to rare plants. Allow 1 hour to explore.

❷ Cave Stream Scenic Reserve and Cave Walk
The landscape of this semi-alpine reserve is dominated by karst rock formations which can be observed along the 30-minute track to the upstream entrance of the main feature – a 594-metre-long cave. If walking though the cave it is recommended to start at the downstream end. The passage through the cave twists and turns, with several small waterfalls to negotiate. It is suitable for inexperienced adult cavers with reasonable fitness, strong footwear and suitably warm clothing, but be ready to get wet up to your waist. There is no light in the cave so bring reliable, waterproof headlamps. Don't enter the cave if there has been recent rain, the water is discoloured or is at a higher level than normal. Allow 1 hour to walk through the cave.

❸ Lake Pearson and Lake Grasmere
These very scenic little lakes are popular for trout fishing in season. Lake Pearson is a great spot for picnics, canoeing and a spot of bird-watching. On a calm day the reflections of the mountains behind can be quite impressive.

❹ DOC Visitor Centre
Located in the Arthur's Pass village, here you will find detailed track information, weather advice, and displays that cover the human and natural history of the Arthur's Pass area.

❺ Devil's Punchbowl Walk
At the northern end of the Arthur's Pass village, on the right hand side, a small road leads to a carpark from where the track begins. After crossing two footbridges, the undulating track leads through beech forest up a narrow valley to the 133-metre-high Devil's Punchbowl waterfall. Allow 1.5 hours return.

❻ Bridal Veil Nature Walk
This track starts from the same carpark as the Devil's Punchbowl walk, at the northern end of the village. Cross the first footbridge then turn left into the beech forest where signposted. Although the track is fairly flat, about halfway along there is a short, steep dip into a gorge cut by Bridal Veil Creek. After climbing back out of the gorge the track continues until it meets the road. Allow 1.5 hours return.

❼ Dobson Nature Walk
This easy 30-minute loop track starts just opposite the Dobson Memorial on the eastern side of Arthur's Pass summit. The easy track wanders through the alpine vegetation which consists of native herbs, shrubs, tussock and mosses. A small booklet about the plant life is available from the DOC office at Arthur's Pass.

❽ Avalanche Peak–Scotts Track Circuit
For those with good fitness this circuit offers good views from above the tree-line of the surrounding mountains. Allow 7–8 hours and be ready for steep sections as you will climb 1000 metres to the summit of Avalanche Peak. The formed track reduces to a route marked with poles and should only be attempted in fine weather. A route guide is available from DOC.

❾ Summit of Arthur's Pass
Just west of the summit you will find a turnoff to Death's Corner Lookout. From here you can look down the valley upon the impressive Otira Viaduct. This viaduct now carries the road past a constantly-shifting section of the hillside which was vulnerable to avalanche – hence the name 'Death's Corner'. The native kea, a mountain parrot, can often be seen and heard flying around the area. Between November and January you are likely to see the native forest around Arthur's Pass festooned with the red flowers of rata trees.

Lake
Coleridge

SH73 to the
WEST COAST

Klondyke
Corner

Avalanche Peak   8

Mt Rolleston

Bealey River

Scott's Track

Arthur's Pass
DOC   4
Devil's Punchbowl
                   5
Bridal Veil Walk
                   6
Dobson Nature Walk   7   Arthur's
                           Pass

Death's Corner
Lookout   9

Mingha River

Otira Viaduct

Otira

Deception River

Otira River

TASMAN SEA

Mt Sefton

SEALY RANGE

Sealy Tarns

9

Kea Point

8

to Hooker Valley

White Horse Hill Camp

3

Sebastopol

DOC
The Hermitage
Mountaineers Cafe/Bar

2
1

7 **10**

Mount Cook Village

Red Tarns

6

SH80 to
TWIZEL
CHRISTCHURCH

Hooker River

Tasman River

4 Mount Cook Airport

At a height of 3754m (12,316 ft) the towering Aoraki/Mt Cook dominates the hundreds of peaks and glaciers that make up New Zealand's Southern Alps. First climbed in 1894 by three New Zealanders, Aoraki remains a formidable challenge for experienced mountaineers. For other visitors, the snow-covered peaks form a wonderful backdrop for walks and outdoor activities. The Mount Cook lily (the world's largest buttercup), the snow gentian and the mountain ribbonwood contrast their white flowers against the surrounding greenery. Native birds commonly seen are the kea, kereru, tomtit, rifleman and harrier hawk.

The main highway into the park passes alongside Lake Pukaki and gives views of the 27-km-long Tasman Glacier. This glacier, the longest glacier in the Southern Hemisphere, is up to 3 km wide and can be 600 metres deep in places.

① The Old Mountaineers' Café & Bar

At the end of a busy day in the outdoors, enjoy a warm fire and a warm welcome at this bustling café, bar and restaurant. Complete with hearty New Zealand meals big enough to quell a mountain-sized appetite. Capturing the spirit of a mountaineer's hut and featuring historic climbing gear and photographs, it is open for breakfast, lunch and dinner.

② DOC Visitor Centre

Exhibits of flora and fauna from throughout the park are displayed alongside a collection of climbing equipment used by famous early mountaineers. You will also find details of local walks and climbs, as well as weather forecasts and a short audio-visual presentation. A programme of walks and talks is arranged during summer and public holidays.

③ Hooker Valley Track

This is the most popular local track, as it is reasonably flat and highly scenic. From the White Horse Hill camping/parking area, it heads up the Hooker Valley towards the magnificent south face of Aoraki/Mt Cook. Times one way from the parking area are: first swingbridge 15 minutes; second swingbridge 30 minutes; Hooker Lake 1.5 hours.

④ Scenic Flights

For an incomparable perspective of the Southern Alps a scenic flight will skim over the glacial ice, dip into side valleys, and even cross the Main Divide to the West Coast glaciers. Ski-planes can land on the snow on the upper reaches of the glaciers.

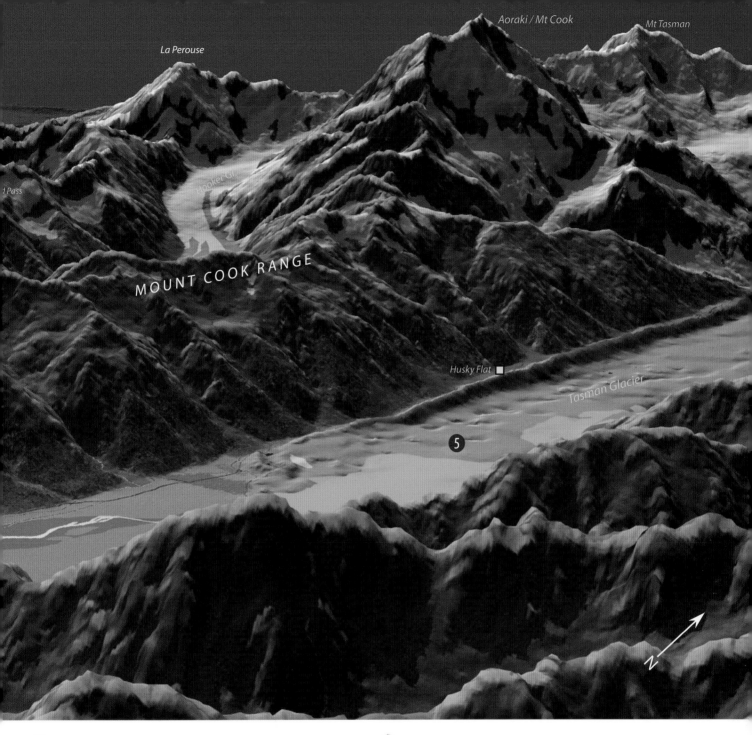

La Perouse

Aoraki / Mt Cook

Mt Tasman

Hooker Gl

1 Pass

MOUNT COOK RANGE

Husky Flat ■

Tasman Glacier

⑤

N

⑤ Guided Trips to Tasman Glacier

Alpine Guides run 2-hour trips from the village to Husky Flat where visitors may climb the moraine wall to look down onto the Tasman Glacier. Glacier Explorers take visitors for an interpretive small-boat trip on the terminal lake at the face of the Tasman Glacier. During summer icebergs are seen floating in the lake, and in winter the lake freezes over.

⑥ Red Tarns Track

This track starts from the public shelter. Follow the path to Black Birch Stream, cross the bridge and then climb steeply to the Red Tarns, which were named after the red weed growing in them. From the viewpoint the valley and Aoraki/Mt Cook create a spectacular panorama.

⑦ Governors Bush Walk

This delightful walk starting by the public shelter explores a stand of beech forest, home to native birdlife, as it climbs gradually to a lookout point before descending back to the village. Allow 1 hour return.

⑧ Kea Point Walk

This walk can be started from the Hermitage lawn (cross the road to the track sign, 2 hours return) or drive to the White Horse Hill parking area (1 hour return). The track wanders its way gently through subalpine tussockland scrub and ends at a platform giving stunning views of Mt Sefton, the Hooker Valley, Mueller Lake and Aoraki/Mt Cook.

⑨ Sealy Tarns Track

Take the Kea Point Track then branch off where signposted for the steep climb up to the tarns (4 hours return). This energetic walk provides spectacular views of the Hooker Valley, Aoraki/Mt Cook and many other peaks. In summer the alpine flowers and views make this uphill hike worth the effort.

⑩ Bowen Bush Walk

This easy 10-minute walk starts opposite Alpine Guides and leads through a small forest of celery pine and totara.

MACKENZIE COUNTRY

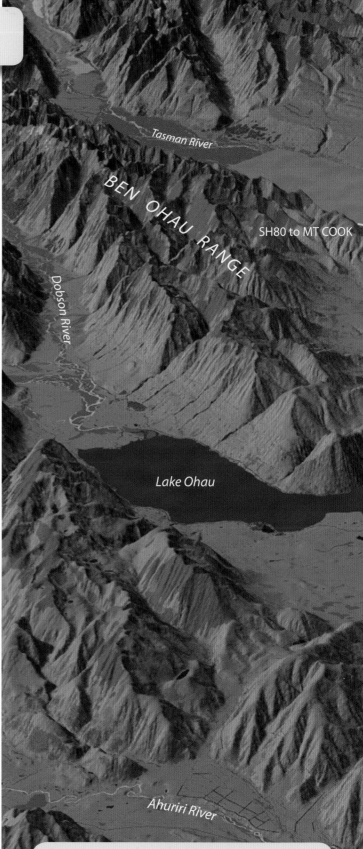

Surrounded by snow-covered mountains, the high, flat terrain of this area is best described as New Zealand's Big Sky Country. SH 8 takes you through South Canterbury and past Aoraki/Mt Cook to the Queenstown Lakes District and is therefore a popular touring route.

Mackenzie Country is named after a rascal of a Scotsman who decided that other people's sheep would contribute greatly to his own farming ambitions. James Mackenzie, with the assistance of a sheepdog called Friday, reputedly rustled some sheep from a big farm near Timaru and drove them inland to the area that now bears his name.

The shallow braided rivers of the Mackenzie Country caused local farmer Bill Hamilton to invent the jet-propulsion system used today by watercraft large and small around the world.

1 Lake Tekapo Village
This small village overlooking Lake Tekapo caters for travellers with shops, petrol, cafés, restaurants and a pub. A good selection of accommodation is available including hotels, motels, hostels and Bed and Breakfasts. Scenic flights take off from here to visit Aoraki/Mt Cook and the Southern Alps. The newest attractions in town are the Winter Park hot pools (open year-round) and outdoor ice rink (in winter).

2 Church of the Good Shepherd
This tiny, charming, stone-built church on the lakeshore was built in 1935 as a memorial to the pioneers who endured early hardship to settle what was remote, tough country with a harsh winter climate. Through the panorama-sized window behind the altar is an impressive view of the lake and snow-capped mountains far beyond.

3 Monument to the Sheepdog
A few metres from the Church of the Good Shepherd stands a bronze sculpture of a sheepdog as a memorial to the loyal, hard-working dogs whose assistance made it possible for this mountainous area to be farmed.

4 Mt John Observatory
The observatory at the top of Mt John is within view of Lake Tekapo village. It was built here for the incredibly clear atmosphere and absence of light pollution from urban sources. A local company called Earth and Sky operates informative guided tours during daytime to visit the many telescopes, view the sun through a special scope and explain the research carried out here. Night tours enable you to view the stars and planets through the telescopes.

5 Lake Pukaki Lookout
At the southern end of Lake Pukaki it is worth stopping, on a fine day, to admire the classic view of Aoraki/Mt Cook rearing up at the end of the lake.

6 Mount Cook Salmon
If you like the taste of fresh or smoked salmon this short diversion off SH 8 will provide a salmon-snacking opportunity. Between Lakes Pukaki and Tekapo signs point to a salmon farm established on a hydro canal. The Mount Cook Salmon Company pioneered the farming of salmon on hydro canals with Chinook and Sockeye salmon originally introduced from Canada.

7 Omarama Village and Gliding
Omarama is a small settlement located at the intersection of SH 8 and SH 83 to Oamaru. Cafés, shops and accommodation are available here but the outstanding attraction has to be the opportunity to try gliding. The position of the Southern Alps affects the predominantly westerly winds making Omarama one of the best gliding locations in the world. Enjoy a lesson with a professional local pilot.

8 Black Stilt / Kaki Guided Tours
Due to habitat loss, predation by introduced pests and disturbance from riverbed recreation, the black stilt is now critically endangered and restricted to the rivers of the Mackenzie basin. DOC runs a protection and breeding programme which is having some success. Viewing the stilts, the breeding facility and many other wading bird species is only possible by joining one of the twice-daily guided tours (duration 1 hour, summer only). Advance booking is essential – contact the Twizel Information Centre.

SH79 to
GERALDINE

Fairlie

SH8 to
TIMARU

Lake Tekapo

Mount John
Observatory

4

1 **2** **3**

Lake Tekapo

Church of the Good Shepherd
Sheepdog Monument

Burkes Pass

hydro canal

6

Mount Cook
Salmon

MARY RANGE

Lake Pukaki

Lake Pukaki

5

Pukaki River

Tekapo River

hydro canal

Twizel

Lake
Ruataniwha

8

Lake Benmore

BENMORE RANGE

Lake Benmore

SH83 to KUROW

Omarama

7

SH8 to
LINDIS PASS
CENTRAL OTAGO

N

WANAKA

Wanaka is the quieter alternative to Queenstown's bustling activity, but still has everything you could wish for in an alpine holiday town. Located at the southern end of Lake Wanaka, this area was first settled by gold miners in the 1870s. The first tourists arrived not long after, attracted by the natural features of what is now Mount Aspiring National Park. Like Queenstown, Wanaka is a year-round destination thanks to the sunny, warm Central Otago summer and nearby skifields for winter fun.

The shimmering waters of Lake Wanaka will first draw your attention on arrival. After dipping your toes in the lake retire to a nearby café for coffee, cake or ice-cream. Research the multitude of outdoor activities on offer but don't make any decisions without a glass of excellent Pinot Noir from one of the local wineries.

1 Visitor Information Centre and DOC Office
The Visitor Information Centre is located right on the waterfront and is a great source of information about the region's attractions and services. For information on Mount Aspiring National Park and the multitude of hiking opportunities visit the DOC office on Ardmore Street, on the corner of Ballantyne Road.

2 Mount Iron Walking Track
Mount Iron is a massive 240-metre-high rock that withstood the grinding action of glaciers during the last ice age. Wide-ranging views are the reward for reaching the top. Very close to Wanaka township, you can access the track near Puzzling World. The track crosses farmland before entering manuka scrub. Allow 1.5 hours for the round trip.

3 Puzzling World
Stuart Landsborough's Puzzling World has been entertaining, confusing and amazing people since 1973. It started with a three-dimensional maze then grew to include a puzzle centre, hologram hall, illusion rooms and a leaning tower. Lots of fun for all ages.

4 The Paradiso Cinema, Café and Bar
This is no ordinary cinema. Recent releases and movies of various genres are presented in this classic old cinema, where your seating may be couches, modified cars, and a variety of other comfy chairs. Beer, wine and great food is available for consumption during the screening.

5 New Zealand Fighter Pilots Museum
The museum is home to an extensive collection of well maintained and airworthy fighter aircraft from WW II. Photographic displays, personal records of fighter pilots, memorabilia and audio-visual presentations give an incredible insight into the history of New Zealand's contribution to the air war over Europe and Asia. You can take a scenic flight in a restored vintage Tiger Moth. Also, right next door is the Transport and Toy museum, with a huge variety of exhibits to interest all ages and genders.

6 Scenic Flights
Wanaka airport is the starting point for scenic flights around Mount Aspiring National Park, or to Milford Sound, Doubtful Sound, Aoraki/Mt Cook and numerous glaciers. Flights can include snow landings or combine with Milford Sound cruises.

7 Local Wanaka Walking Tracks
Full details are available from DOC. The Roys Peak track begins 5 minutes drive west from Wanaka. The view from the top includes most of the lake and across to Mt Aspiring/Tititea. Allow 3 hours each way. For the Diamond Lake and Rocky Hill Track drive 25 minutes west along the Mt Aspiring road then turn right where the sign indicates. This track involves a steady climb to the lake, then beyond to the Rocky Hill summit for grand views all around. Allow 1.5 hours each way.

8 Matukituki Valley Walks
The Matukituki Valley is in Mount Aspiring National Park, an hours drive west from Wanaka (on unsealed road beyond Treble Cone skifield), and offers some great day-walk options. The Rob Roy Track is very popular, requiring 3–4 hours (return) with some steep sections on the way up to close views of Rob Roy Glacier. From the roadend carpark to Mt Aspiring Hut is a gentle 2.5 hours one way through farmland and native vegetation. Mt Aspiring Hut is a popular base from which to explore further up the valley. Continue another 1.5 hours to Pearl Flat or 2 hours to the head of the valley. Purchase DOC brochures for full information.

9 Canyoning Adventures
The steep, forested valleys and plunging waterfalls of Mount Aspiring National Park are perfect for the climbing, swimming, abseiling and floating involved in Deep Canyon Wanaka's 'canyoning' adventures. These are active trips suitable for people with average fitness who are confident in water and have a sense of adventure. Trips start from the Wanaka base between November and March.

MOUNT ASPIRING NATIONAL PARK

SH6 to HAAST
WEST COAST

Makarora River

Lake Wanaka

Lake Hawea

Glendhu Bay

Roys Peak

7

Lake
Hawea

Mt Iron

2

4

1

Wanaka

3

Puzzling World

Clutha River

Cardrona Valley Rd

SH6 to
CROMWELL

6

Wanaka Airport

5

NZ Fighter
Pilots Museum

ARROWTOWN & THE KAWARAU GORGE

The Arrow River became the focus of a gold rush in 1862, causing a town of more than 7000 people to flourish along the Arrow riverbank. After the gold was extracted the town all but closed down, only reviving itself in the late 20th century thanks to the growing visitor industry. Today the population stands at around 1800 people. The historic buildings are preserved by local regulation and occupied by shops, galleries and cafés, making this a very pleasant town to explore on foot.

❶ Lakes District Museum, Arrowtown
This museum presents the human history of the region, going back over 1200 years of Maori exploration, the first sheep farm settlements, the boom times of the Arrow and Shotover gold strikes, Chinese immigration and political issues.

❷ Chinese Settlement
The most unfortunate participants in the 1860s gold rush were the Chinese miners and businessmen. Victims of discrimination and shunned by the Europeans, they struggled to get ahead. Three minutes from the western end of town, alongside Bush Creek, are the remnants of the Chinese settlement. The remaining huts have been protected and restored, and the Chinese settlers' stories explained by way of interpretive panels.

❸ The Lord of the Rings Film Sites
Arrowtown has been the filming location for a number of movies, most famously The Lord of the Rings. Close to Arrowtown can be found 'The Ford of Bruinen' and 'Gladden Fields'. Further away, by the Kawarau River, are the locations for 'Pillars of the Kings' and 'River Anduin'.

❹ Wineries
The climate of Central Otago ranges from hot summers to very cold winters – not so good for the early gold miners. Despite the first vine being planted in the 1860s the wine industry did not become established until the late 1980s. Today some of the world's best Pinot Noir comes from Central Otago. There are more wineries here than you could ever hope to visit, but do visit as many as you can, either on your own or with a tour, for wine-tasting and buying, and a café lunch amongst the vines.

❺ Kawarau Bridge Bungy Jump
This is where commercial bungy-jumping began – inspired by the vine-jumping tradition on the South Pacific island of Vanuatu. The first bungy operation began on the historic Kawarau Bridge in 1988, and spawned an adrenaline-pumping business that now spans the globe. Whether you try the 43-metre jump over the Kawarau River or just enjoy watching the thrill-seekers leaping off, it's an interesting place to visit.

❻ Kawarau Gorge
Lake Wakatipu's only river outlet flows through the rugged Kawarau Gorge to Cromwell. The river, with a few grade 2–3 rapids, is the location for white-water rafting and river-boarding trips. At the Goldfields Mining Centre you can explore the tailings and relics from gold mining days, pan for gold and observe an operating stamper battery.

❼ Historic Macetown
Macetown sprang to life when gold miners worked the upper reaches of the Arrow River. It is now a ghost town, but the remaining stone buildings and stamper batteries have been restored. Macetown can be reached by walking the Big Hill Trail (allow 5–6 hours), driving the 4WD track with its many river crossings, or joining a guided 4WD tour. The Arrowtown Museum has further information on this and other local walks.

❽ Crown Range Road
The road over the Crown Range to Wanaka is 52 km long and is the highest main road in New Zealand. From the Arrow Junction the road zigzags steeply to a saddle 1119 m above sea-level. Along the way you can enjoy spectacular views of Arrowtown, the Kawarau Gorge and as far as Lake Wakatipu. Continue down the Cardrona Valley for the Cardrona skifield, historic Cardrona Hotel and the Waiorau Snow Farm, which provides cross-country skiing, hiking and biking.

❾ Cardrona Hotel
Perhaps the most renowned country pub in New Zealand, the historic Cardrona Hotel was established in 1863 when gold fever was rife in the region. The warm beer of the 1860s has been replaced by colder varieties but it is still served across the same bar. It is situated in the Cardrona Valley, beside the Wanaka–Queenstown road.

to WANAKA

■ Cardrona Skifield

Cardrona River

■ Waiorau Snow Farm

Cardrona Hotel ⑨

CROWN RANGE

⑧

CROWN TERRACE

Kawarau Bridge Bungy

er

⑤

④ Gibbston ☐

⑥ SH6 to
CROMWELL

Goldfields Mining Centre
Kawarau Gorge

QUEENSTOWN

What a town! Your first impression of Queenstown will be of spectacular geography: high, craggy mountains surrounding a long, white-capped lake. Your second impression will be of the energy that emanates from this busy holiday centre from dawn until after dark. The natural features of this region have enabled the local people's enthusiasm for outdoor adventure to slip into overdrive.

Besides the adrenaline sports, Queenstown can also be a great place for culture, cuisine, history and the creative arts. The gold-rush period of the 1800s destroyed most of the area's native forest but there are still interesting walking tracks and quiet, scenic spots for escaping the modern Queenstown 'rush'.

❶ Information Centre and Booking Offices
At the intersection of Shotover and Camp streets you will find several booking agencies and the official i-Site visitor centre, which is the best source for information on nearly everything in the greater Queenstown, Wanaka and Fiordland areas.

❷ Queenstown Gardens and Lakeside Walk
This is an enjoyable park with tall, established exotic trees, lawns and a variety of flowerbeds. Explore the gardens, or walk the 20–30 minute lakeside track that begins beside the Queenstown beach, does a circuit around the gardens and returns over the peninsula.

❸ Queenstown Hill Track
Climb the hill behind town, via Beetham and Edgar streets, to find the signposted track up Queenstown Hill. This steep track takes you through pine forest before reaching open farmland and provides excellent views of Lake Wakatipu. Allow 2–2.5 hours return.

❹ Frankton Arm Walkway
This is an easy and enjoyable lakeside walk that can be started from Queenstown beach (to include a circuit of the Gardens) or from the end of Park Street. Walking the full track will take you all the way to Frankton in 1–2 hours one way.

❺ Skyline Gondola
The easy way to get high above Queenstown is to ride the gondola from the end of Brecon Street. At the top you will find fabulous views, a restaurant, Maori cultural show, bungy jump, big swing and luge activities. Hiking opportunities start from here. There are three ways back down – via the gondola again, down the One Mile Creek track (1.5 hours), or make like a bird and hitch yourself to a paragliding pilot.

❻ Golf Courses
The surrounding alpine landscape makes a great backdrop for a game of golf. Close to Queenstown are the 18-hole Kelvin Heights course and the 9-hole Frankton Golf Course and driving range.

7 Kiwi and Birdlife Park
Located on Brecon Street just below the base of the gondola, with good opportunities to view kiwi and other native flora and fauna. Kiwi feeding takes place at 1.30 pm daily. A conservation show takes place at 11 am, 1.30 pm and 3 pm daily, where a zoologist introduces you to some of New Zealand's native species. Open (roughly) between 9 am and 7 pm (6 pm during winter).

8 Arthurs Point
Six km from central Queenstown at Arthurs Point you will find a quiet tavern favoured by the locals, an historic bridge over the Shotover River, the base for Shotover Jet's jet-boat rides up the river, horse treks and perhaps the most renowned restaurant in the region – Gantley's, a fine-dining experience beyond compare.

9 Ben Lomond Track
If Queenstown Hill and the Skyline Complex are not high enough for you try hiking up Ben Lomond, located up behind Bobs Peak. Start from the lakefront on the One Mile Creek track or from the top of the gondola. The route is steep, so good fitness is required. Allow 4 hours (return) to the saddle or 7–8 hours (return) to the summit.

10 Lake Dispute
Ten km from Queenstown, along the road to Glenorchy, is the beginning of the track to Lake Dispute. Start with a steep climb, allowing 35–45 minutes to reach the lake.

Continue alongside Lake Dispute and down into the Moke Lake Recreation Reserve for 2 hours to reach Moke Lake.

11 Moke Lake
Drive along Moke Lake Road (turn off 8 km from Queenstown) to reach this slightly larger lake fringed by several wetlands. Allow 1.5 hours to walk around it.

12 Coronet Peak
Only 30 minutes from Arrowtown or Queenstown, Coronet Peak is busiest during winter when it becomes a 280-ha skifield. During January and February the chairlifts operate for hikers, sightseers and mountain-bikers to catch a ride to the top of the mountain. Mountain bikes are available for hire (book in advance).

13 The Remarkables Mountain Range
In winter The Remarkables are covered with snow and snow-bunnies, but during summer the snow retreats, allowing the tussock-covered slopes and walking tracks to emerge. From Queenstown to the skifield buildings is a 45-minute drive via the unsealed skifield access road. From the carpark you can walk into Shadow Basin then up to the ridgeline for a stunning view of Lake Wakatipu, Queenstown and the surrounding mountains (3 hours return). A second option is to visit Lake Alta, created by glacial action and providing a glacial-temperature swimming opportunity (allow 1.5–2 hours return).

GLENORCHY

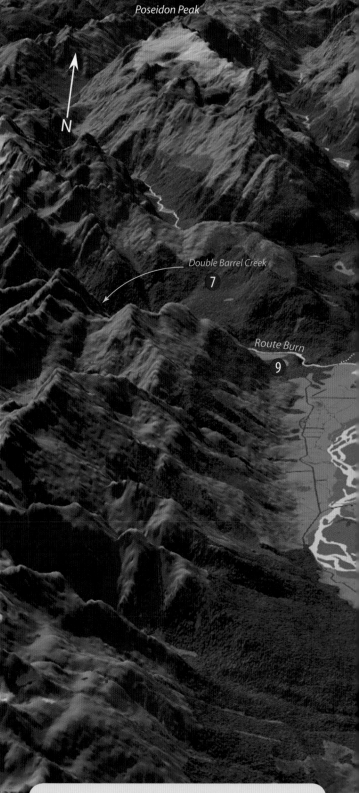

Poseidon Peak

N

Double Barrel Creek

7

Route Burn

9

Venture beyond the thrill-rides and cafés of Queenstown to the northern end of Lake Wakatipu and you will find Glenorchy, a small town quietly enjoying its stunning alpine wilderness location. Glenorchy can be a great day-trip from Queenstown but, if you have the time and love to explore nature, you could easily spend a few nights here. The drive alongside Lake Wakatipu takes around 45 minutes and reveals a natural feast for your eyes. Beyond Glenorchy are the peaks of Mount Aspiring National Park. This is the New Zealand scenery that draws film crews from all over the world.

❶ Glenorchy Village

Quiet and secluded, Glenorchy has most of the facilities you might need: local store, petrol, bar, cafés, craft shops, several wilderness activity operators, and the Department of Conservation visitor centre. At the western end of town you will find a picnic area with public toilets. Supplies for multi-day hikes are best purchased back in Queenstown.

❷ Designer Fur Fashion

You can do your bit for conservation by purchasing a warm fur-lined jacket or vest from the Glenorchy Fur Products shop. Garments are manufactured locally using the fur from brush-tailed possums – these introduced animals are a serious ecological threat to the New Zealand wilderness.

❸ Glenorchy Wetland Walkway

From the pier at the western end of town you can begin an easy walk along the shoreline and up Lagoon Creek to the Glenorchy Lagoon (30–45 minutes). A flat track continues around the lagoon, with boardwalks over wetland areas. Vegetation is mainly exotic but you have a good chance of viewing redpoll, swans, geese, ducks and other birdlife. The walkway loop can also be accessed from the top of Oban Street and by itself takes around an hour.

❹ Kinloch

This small settlement is focused around the Kinloch Lodge where you will find moderately-priced accommodation and a restaurant. A transfer service takes hikers to and from all the major tracks. There is also a DOC campsite here.

❺ Dart River Safaris

This well-established company offers excursions into the wilderness north of Glenorchy by jet-boat or 'Fun Yak' inflatable canoes. During their trips you will explore the Dart River, take a short hike in the native forest and have a picnic lunch. No experience is necessary, but bookings are recommended.

❻ Lake Sylvan Walk

Lake Sylvan is 30 minutes drive from Glenorchy on some unsealed roads. From the carpark cross a small swingbridge, then enter tall native beech forest on the way to Lake Sylvan. Allow 45 minutes each way to reach the lake. Return the same way or make a loop around the old tramline which involves getting your feet wet during a small river crossing. Allow 1.5–2 hours for the loop.

❼ Double Barrel Creek

Park near the Routeburn shelter, at the beginning of the 2–3 day Routeburn Track. The Double Barrel Creek walk is a very easy 30-minute loop track featuring beautiful native forest and great views.

❽ Diamond Creek to Lake Reid and Diamond Lake

Park beside Diamond Creek and walk upstream with the creek on your left. The track as far as Lake Reid is pretty good but can be a little soft underfoot when wet (allow 30 minutes one way). The track from Lake Reid to Diamond Lake is pretty rough and takes another 30 minutes, with good views all around. Ducks and trout frequent this waterway, which is popular with fishermen.

❾ A Feast of Multi-day Hiking

Near Glenorchy you will find a number of popular multi-day hikes. The Routeburn, Greenstone and Caples tracks are each 2–3 days long, or you can combine two of them together as a loop track over 4–5 days. The Rees and Dart (4–5 days) tracks are normally done as a loop.

❿ Scenic Flights

From the small Glenorchy airstrip you can enjoy scenic flights to Milford Sound, Aoraki/Mt Cook, the West Coast glaciers and a number of even more isolated spots such as Stewart Island and remote beaches along the Fiordland National Park coastline.

Mt Earnslaw/Pikirakatahi

Dart River / Te Awa Whakatipu

Rees River

MOUNT ASPIRING NATIONAL PARK

9

Lake Sylvan

6

■ Paradise

Mt Alfred/Ari

Diamond Lake

Lake Reid

8

Diamond Ck

River / Te Awa Whakatipu

Rees River

5

4 ■ Kinloch

Glenorchy Lagoon

3

2 **1** Glenorchy

Lake Wakatipu

to QUEENSTOWN

10

TE ANAU, MANAPOURI & DOUBTFUL SOUND

Doubtful Sound
6

Manapouri Underground
Power Station
8

KEPLER
MOUNTAINS

West Arm

Lake Manapouri

Hope Arm

7

Back Valley
Hut

Waiau R.

Manapouri

5 Pearl Harbour

SH95

For exploring Milford Sound, Doubtful Sound and the more remote parts of Fiordland National Park at a relaxed pace, base yourself in Te Anau or Manapouri. The natural attractions of the Fiordland World Heritage Area are obvious. Don't rush through, but spend a whole day on a trip to Milford or Doubtful sounds, or preferably both with an overnight stay. Take the time to experience the other possibilities in this area as well. Fiordland is at its best when the mountaintops are bathed in sunshine, waterfalls cascade down the fiord walls during a storm, or its valleys are buried in a blanket of snow. There is little chance of seeing all these in one day, but the longer you stay the more you can appreciate the moods of this raw, powerful, beautiful place. This is a true rainforest area – if it's wet, put on your raincoat and a positive attitude and go for it!

1 Te Anau Lakefront Walk
A flat, well-formed path follows the Te Anau lakeshore. From the i-Site information centre turn right and walk for 90 minutes to the Upukerora River, or turn left and walk along to the DOC visitor centre (5 minutes), Wildlife Park (15–20 minutes), and Control Gates (1 hour) – all times one way. The Control Gates are associated with the Lake Manapouri underground power station, regulating the flow of water between the lakes. Beyond the Control Gates is the Kepler Track, the first parts of which can be walked in one day – a water taxi can save walking back the same way.

2 Te Anau Wildlife Centre
Here you can observe a variety of New Zealand's native bird species such as the takahe, weka, and parakeets, some housed in aviaries and others just visiting. Birds held in the aviaries are either recovering after an injury or participating in a breeding programme. Open during daylight hours, with entry by gold coin donation.

3 Ata Whenua – Shadowlands Movie
This half-hour movie of Fiordland's spectacular scenery was filmed by a local helicopter company. The film shows you parts of the national park only accessible by air, and conveys the differences that a change in weather or season brings. The cinema is located in The Lane, central Te Anau, and mainstream movies are also screened.

4 Te Ana-au Glow-worm Caves
Located on the opposite side of Lake Te Anau, this limestone cave system is reached by launch during a 2.5-hour guided excursion. Inside the cave you can observe the

FIORDLAND
NATIONAL PARK

MURCHISON MOUNTAINS

Middle Fiord

Kepler Track

South Fiord

4 *Te Ana-au Caves*

Lake Te Anau

Kepler Track

control gates

DOC

1 Te Anau

3

2

Wildlife
Centre

9

SH94 to
MILFORD

SH94 to
QUEENSTOWN

Upukerora River

N

limestone formations, small waterfalls and native glow-worms. With well-formed paths and handrails this activity is suitable for people of all ages and fitness levels. Take warm clothing as it can be quite cool in the cave.

5 Manapouri Township
This smaller town sits on the shore of Lake Manapouri and has several accommodation and café/restaurant options. Manapouri is the second-deepest lake in New Zealand. During the 1960s a campaign by conservationists forced the Manapouri power station to keep the level of the lake within its natural range. Manapouri is the starting point for excursions to Doubtful Sound and the Dusky Track.

6 Doubtful Sound
Doubtful Sound is one of the longest fiords in New Zealand, and with the floor of the fiord 420 m below the surface, it's also the deepest. In comparison to Milford Sound, the surrounding mountains are not as high but the isolation is greater and cruising duration is longer. Various operators take day and multi-day trips for cruising, wildlife viewing, kayaking and fishing. Trips usually depart from Pearl Harbour at the southern end of Manapouri township.

7 Manapouri Walks
Water taxis or rowboats for hire can take you from Pearl Harbour across the Waiau River, from where several hiking options begin. The Circle Track has steep sections during its 3.5-hour circuit. Several other options reach Hope Arm Hut or head inland to Back Valley Hut. Get advice from DOC about the weather and track conditions before starting.

8 Manapouri Underground Power Station
This hydro-power station is located deep underground, hewn from the solid rock beneath the mountains of Fiordland. Water from Lake Manapouri travels through massive pipes to the turbines in the machine hall near the outlet at Doubtful Sound. You can join a trip to the power station, accessed first by cruising across the lake then by coach down a 2 km spiral tunnel.

9 Multi-day Tracks and Track Transport
This area is hikers' heaven: the Milford, Kepler, Routeburn, Caples, Greenstone, Hollyford and Dusky tracks can all be started from here. Shuttles are available for transport to and from the track ends.

MILFORD ROAD

Most of Fiordland National Park is inaccessible without a helicopter or strong pair of hiking boots, which makes the road to Milford Sound the easiest way to explore this rainforested wilderness. While direct flights to Milford are available, you can make the most of a one-day or overnight visit by beginning your journey in Te Anau. Explore the walking tracks, take in the amazing views and learn about the geological processes and moody climate that have created this truly wonderful, natural environment.

Allow a minimum of 2.5 hours for driving between Te Anau and Milford, and at least another hour or two for stops and short walks. Being the only road it does get busy, so keep an eye on your rear vision mirror. There are no shops, cafés or accommodation between Te Anau and Milford Sound so be sure to plan all your needs before starting off. (See the Milford Sound page for more info on services.)

1 Milford Road picnic spots
On a fine day no café can beat the fresh air and spectacular views along the Milford Road. Grab a picnic lunch and dine at one of the roadside parking areas, where you will find tables and toilets. Be sure to take all your rubbish away with you, and please don't feed the birdlife as some foods can cause them illness and even death.

2 Mirror Lakes
A short boardwalk leads you past several small ponds famous for the reflections of the mountain scenery behind. Best viewed in calm weather.

3 Avenue of the Disappearing Mountain
Travelling between Mirror Lakes and Lake Gunn, the rise of the road creates an optical illusion, as if the mountain in front of you is sinking into the surrounding beech forest.

4 Lake Gunn Nature Walk
Follow a flat, easy loop track through a beech forest full of moss, lichen and native birds to the edge of Lake Gunn, named after an early explorer (30 minutes return).

5 Knobs Flat
An interesting display explains the dynamic nature of the area, including the avalanches that often occur during winter and spring. A telephone is available here if needed (card-phone).

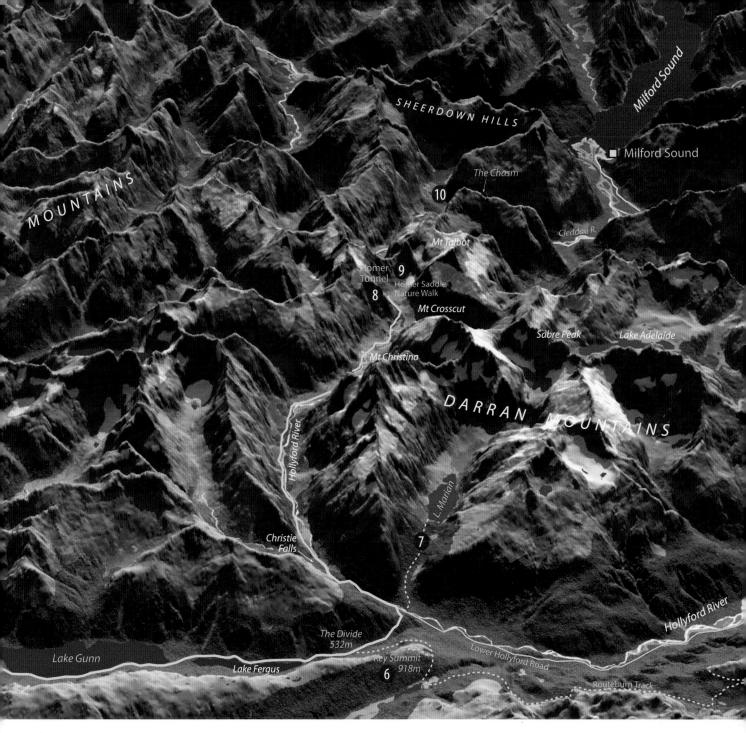

The following labels appear on the map:

Milford Sound

SHEERDOWN HILLS

■ Milford Sound

The Chasm

10

Cleddau R.

Mt Talbot

Homer
Tunnel 9

8 Homer Saddle
Nature Walk

Mt Crosscut

Sabre Peak   *Lake Adelaide*

Mt Christina

D A R R A N   M O U N T A I N S

Hollyford River

L. Marian

M O U N T A I N S

*Christie
Falls*

7

Hollyford River

*The Divide
532m*

Lower Hollyford Road

Lake Gunn

*Key Summit
918m*

Lake Fergus

6

Routeburn Track

6 Key Summit

The first section of the Routeburn Track leads you on a steady uphill walk through silver beech forest to the alpine garden of Key Summit. Above the tree line you will find native shrubs and tussock, prolific birdlife and 360-degree panoramic views of the snow-capped Southern Alps. The track is suitable for people with average fitness – allow 3–4 hours return. It starts from the Divide, where you will find convenient parking, shelter and toilets.

7 Lake Marian Walk

Turn off the Milford Road into the Lower Hollyford Road. After 1 km you will find a carpark and the start of the track. From here cross a swingbridge and take a gentle walk through beech forest to a viewing gantry (1 hour return). The track continues for a further hour to Lake Marian via a much steeper section (which can be muddy after rain), but the scenery is stunning, with the lake in a hanging glacial valley.

8 Homer Tunnel

This 1270-metre tunnel was completed in 1953 and provides access from the Hollyford Valley to the Milford area. Named after William Homer, who discovered the saddle in 1889, the granite walls and ceiling of the tunnel remain unlined. The 1:10 gradient and occasional splash of water on your windscreen make for an interesting passage through. Traffic lights control the traffic during summer.

9 Homer Saddle Nature Walk

On the eastern side of the tunnel you will find stunning views, the occasional cheeky native kea, and an easy nature walk. Start from the parking area to the right of the tunnel and follow the basic loop track (20 minutes return). Stopping near the tunnel is discouraged during winter and spring due to the risk of avalanche.

10 The Chasm Waterfall Walk

A 15–20 minute flat walk takes you through pristine beech forest to where the Cleddau River has carved its way through solid rock, creating several sculpted waterfalls.

MILFORD SOUND

Milford Sound has been New Zealand's most iconic destination since European tourists first arrived in 1890, and rightly so. A true fiord, and the most northern (and arguably most scenic) of the many fiords making up Fiordland National Park the landscape was carved by glacial action over thousands of years. Today, while you cruise the surface of the fiord, the valley floor slumbers 300 m below and the mountain peaks rise vertically over 1,700 m above.

This storm-battered place is a sight to make you gaze skyward in awe, with sheer cliffs, cascading waterfalls, hanging valleys, subtropical rainforest and a variety of marine life. Milford Sound can be enjoyed in any weather. In fact hope for rain, as a heavy rainfall will allow hundreds of waterfalls to emerge and turn the sheer cliffs into a continuous curtain of water.

The services available in Milford Sound are few. Cruise, kayak and scenic flight operations are the focus of life. The only accommodation options are one hostel/backpackers, and a few overnight-cruise boats. If you plan to overnight in Milford Sound we recommend you book in advance.

❶ Blue Duck Pub and Café

Apart from the Milford cruise boats, these are the only options in Milford Sound for meals. The café opens from 8 am (in summer) for breakfast and lunch, closing at 5 pm The pub opens around lunchtime until late, serving hot meals and cold beer. Blue Duck Café also provides internet access and a booking service for local activities. It is located by the main public carpark, 500 metres back from the wharf building.

❷ Milford Sound Lodge

Surrounded by native forest, hungry sandflies and towering mountains, Milford Sound Lodge provides accommodation in the form of private rooms, dorm beds, tent and caravan sites.

❸ Sea Kayaking

Sea kayaking is an incredible way to experience the raw nature and spirit of the fiord, and the only chance to get really close to Milford's native wildlife, which includes seals, dolphins and Fiordland crested penguins. Several companies offer a variety of kayaking options for beginners and the more experienced. All gear and instruction is provided, and pre-booking is essential.

❹ Milford Sound Cruises

The most popular way to view the full 15-km length of this drowned glacial valley is to take a cruise. Several cruise operators pass close by the towering cliffs of sheer rock on the way to the Tasman Sea. Very high annual rainfall gives life to this wild environment, allowing lush rainforest to cling precariously to vertical slopes. Dolphins ride the bow waves, seals and penguins are often visible, and 'tree avalanches' and other features are explained by onboard nature guides.

❺ Milford Deep Underwater Observatory

The unique marine life of Milford Sound is revealed during a visit to Milford Deep. A thick layer of fresh water on the surface blocks light to the saltwater below, and so deep-water species such as corals, anemones, sponges and sea horses can thrive close to the surface. After an introductory talk, you are taken down to the underwater viewing chamber. The observatory is accessible only in conjunction with certain boat cruises.

❻ Scenic flights

Helicopter and fixed-wing aircraft depart from the small but busy Milford airport for scenic flights around Milford Sound and between Milford and Queenstown. Bookings can be made at the Blue Duck Café or inside the Milford wharf building.

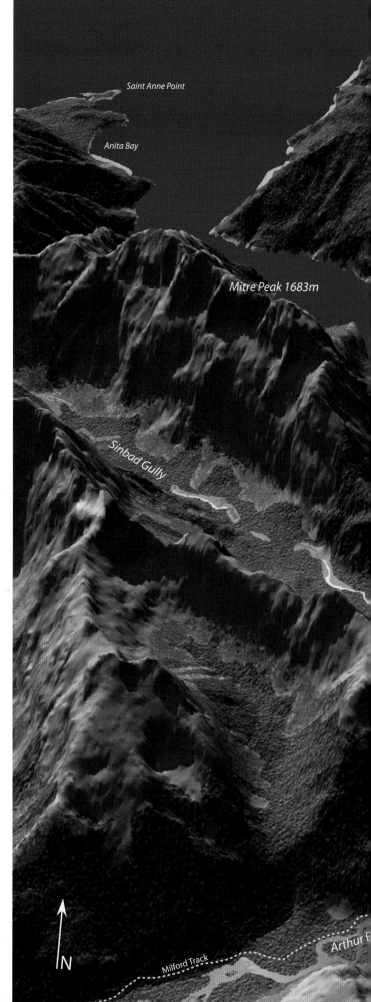

Saint Anne Point

Anita Bay

Mitre Peak 1683m

Sinbad Gully

Milford Track

Arthur F

N

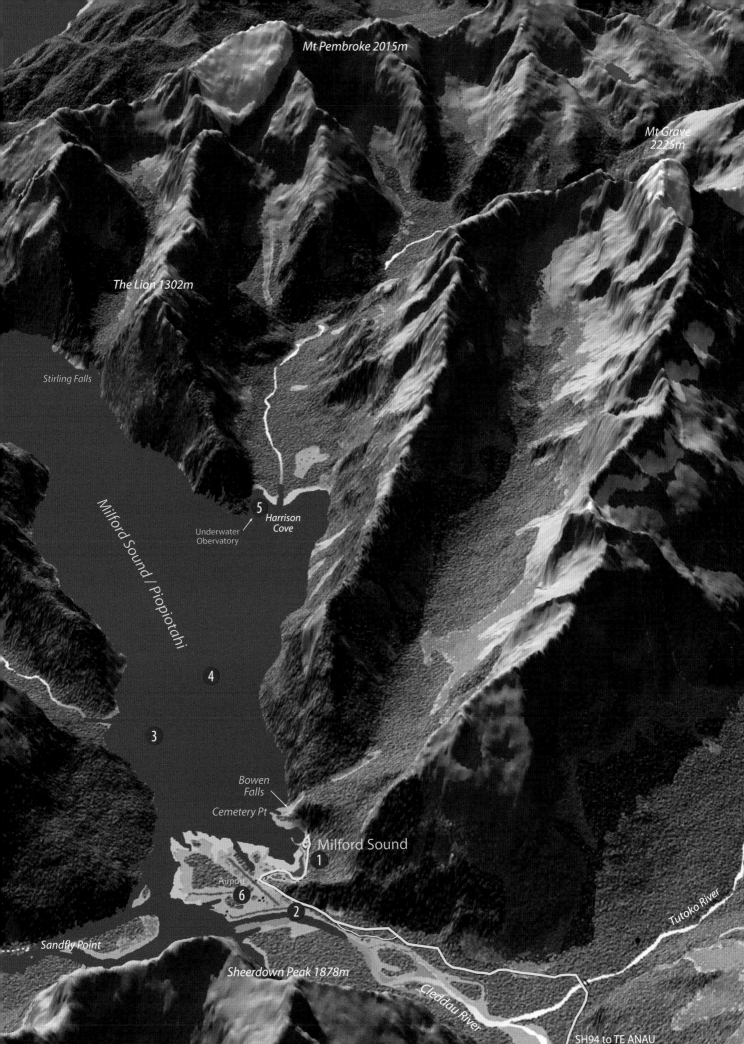

Mt Pembroke 2015m

Mt Grave
2225m

The Lion 1302m

Stirling Falls

5 Harrison
Cove

Underwater
Obervatory

Milford Sound / Piopiotahi

4

3

Bowen
Falls

Cemetery Pt

Milford Sound
1

Airport
6

2

Tutoko River

Sandfly Point

Sheerdown Peak 1878m

Cleddau River

SH94 to TE ANAU

DUNEDIN CITY

Dunedin has something for everyone: wildlife viewing without cages; art galleries and museums; education and amusement; perhaps the finest collection of Victorian/Edwardian architecture in New Zealand: and be sure to visit the University, Railway Station and First Presbyterian Church for exceptional examples. The first inhabitants were the Maori, followed by European whalers and sealers, but the coastal settlement only really began to thrive once the industrious Scottish migrants arrived, bringing their religion and traditions with them to create 'Dun-Edin' – the Edinburgh of the South. The city has enough entertainment for several days, and the Otago Peninsula is well worth visiting in its own right.

❶ Dunedin Public Art Gallery

Dunedin's Public Art Gallery has an outstanding collection of artworks from around the world, some dating back to the 15th century. Alongside the paintings you will find works in other media, including textiles, ceramics and furniture, purchased or bequeathed since the gallery was established in 1884. Located in the Octagon, and open daily between 10 am and 5 pm.

❷ Otago Museum

The Otago Museum is a feast of entertaining and educating galleries, each one themed on different New Zealand, Pacific and world cultures, New Zealand nature and conservation challenges, and our maritime history. Take your time to enjoy all 3 floors of the museum, and the very nice café. Located at 419 Great King Street. Open daily between 10 am and 5 pm

❸ Otago Settlers Museum

This important museum focuses on the social history of Otago, covering the early Maori inhabitants and the other nationalities that have given this city and region its distinctive character. Documents and portraits of early settlers, costumes, household artefacts, local transport and other collections combine to reveal the social fabric of the region through the years. The architecture of the museum buildings is also interesting, with Art Deco and Edwardian styling.

❹ Taieri Gorge Railway

The Central Otago railway from Dunedin to Cromwell originally carried supplies inland and farm produce out to the coast. In 1990, when the railway was closed in favour of road transport, the track between Dunedin and Middlemarch was purchased for train excursions. The Taieri Gorge Railway now attracts thousands of tourists, transporting them across the dramatic Central Otago landscape, through 10 tunnels and over 35 bridges. From Middlemarch people can cycle (4 days) or walk (6 days) to Cromwell along the 150-km Otago Central Rail Trail.

❺ Olveston Historic Home

This stunning Jacobean-style home was built between 1904 and 1906 for David Theomin, a successful businessman. Perhaps the grandest home in Dunedin, there are 35 rooms complete with all the furniture, paintings and possessions collected by the family during their world travels. Bookings are required for the 1-hour guided tours scheduled several times daily (closed Christmas Day).

❻ Speight's Brewery

In 1876 James Speight and several colleagues quit working for a local brewery and set up their own. Starting with an ale, their range of beers has grown, along with the legions of Speight's devotees. During the 90-minute tour you will learn about the origins and ingredients of beer and of course the story of Speight's Brewery itself. Tours are at 10 am, 12 pm and 2 pm daily. Bookings are essential.

❼ Dunedin Botanic Gardens

This 28-ha garden is located at the northern end of the central city. Statues and fountains are spread amongst rhododendrons, roses, camellias, extensive lawns, native New Zealand species and tall trees from all over the world. There is even an aviary with more than 200 birds. Open daily between dawn and dusk.

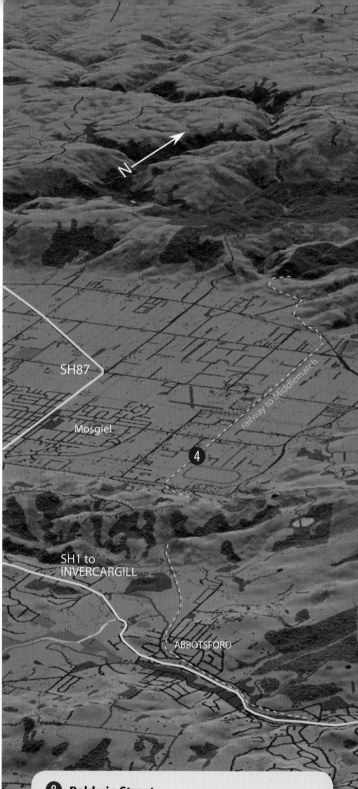

❽ Baldwin Street

Thanks to town planners back in London disregarding the actual terrain, logic was defied and Baldwin Street came to be the steepest street in the world. Constructed from concrete (tar seal would melt and slide downhill on warm days), the gradient is 1:2.86 or 35%.

❾ Cadbury Chocolate Factory

Billing itself as Dunedin's tastiest attraction, a tour (1 hour and 15 minutes) of the Cadbury factory shows you the origins of chocolate, the actual production line and a huge chocolate waterfall. You can sample a few varieties along the way, and of course, at the end of the tour buy as much chocolate as you like. Open between 9 am and 3.15 pm.

railway to
Middlemarch

Taieri Gorge

SILVER PEAKS

*Swampy
Summit*

SH1 to
TIMARU

KAIKORAI

MORNINGTON

Olveston 5
Art Gallery
First Church
Speights Brewery 6
1 Octagon
3
9
CAVERSHAM
Otago Settlers Museum
SOUTH DUNEDIN

NORTH DUNEDIN

Otago Museum
2

Cadbury Chocolate Factory
Railway Station

Otago University

7
Botanic Gardens

NORTH EAST VALLEY

Baldwin St 8

CLAIR

ST KILDA

ANDERSONS BAY

Otago Harbour

Otago Peninsula

Just a short drive from the bustling city of Dunedin is perhaps one of the most important areas for wildlife conservation in New Zealand. Otago Peninsula, created by an extinct volcano, hosted a seal- and whale-hunting industry between 1800 and 1840. When those industries collapsed the wildlife began a slow recovery, and the peninsula is now a valued habitat for diverse species of birdlife, seals, penguins and the occasional sea lion.

There are two roads along the peninsula, providing an enjoyable round trip. Highcliff Road follows the ridgeline then drops down to join the harbourside Portobello Road at the small settlement of Portobello. From here, Harrington Point Road goes all the way to Taiaroa Head.

❶ Royal Albatross Colony

While albatross colonies worldwide are normally on offshore islands, there is a royal albatross colony established on the Otago Peninsula. Intensive pest control measures are required year-round to protect the birds.

Allow 1 hour to drive from the city to Taiaroa Head, at the very end of the peninsula. The visitor centre displays are free to examine and you may spot albatross flying overhead, but to view the birds on their nests you need to join a guided tour.

The tours start with an educational talk and video, then pass through pest-control fences to reach an observatory building. You can also eat at the café, take a tour of the Armstrong Disappearing Gun, wander over to the eastern cliff to see other bird varieties or head down to Pilots Beach to look for seals.

❷ Penguin Place

At Penguin Place, 5 minutes back from Taiaroa Head, coastal farmland has been dedicated to conserving the yellow-eyed penguin, or hoiho. These penguins are the world's rarest, but have slowly increased their numbers thanks to pest control and the creation of nesting boxes. Ninety-minute guided tours start with a 4WD mini-bus trip across the farm, then continue on foot through a network of concealed trenches and shelters.

❸ Larnach Castle

William Larnach, a wealthy businessman and politician, spent a fortune in 1871 creating a unique building that has become known as New Zealand's only castle. Scandal and tragedy struck the family and the castle fell into a sorry state before the present owners restored it. It is located halfway (25 minutes) along the peninsula,

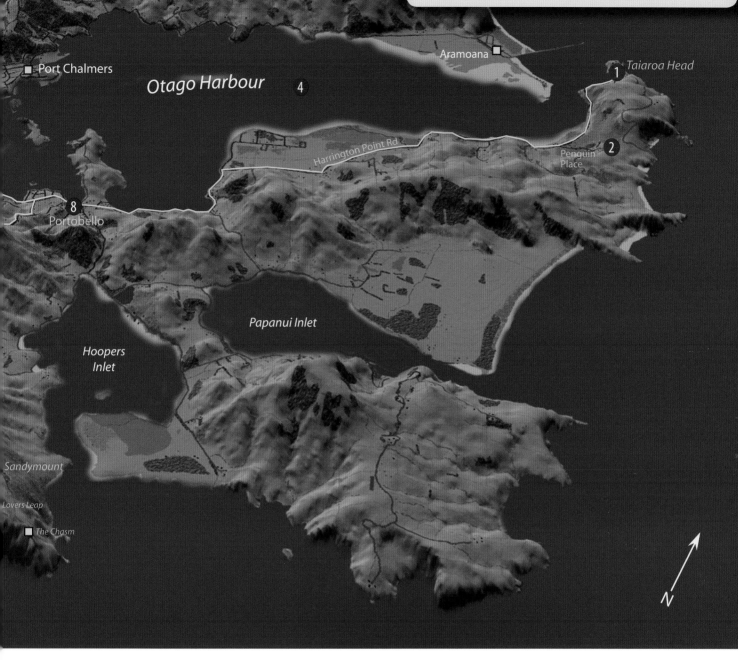

Otago Harbour

Port Chalmers

Aramoana

Taiaroa Head

1

Penguin Place

2

Harrington Point Rd

4

8
Portobello

Papanui Inlet

Hoopers Inlet

Sandymount

Lovers Leap

The Chasm

N

and visitors can take a self-guided tour around the castle and gardens. Their café is open for coffee and lunch, and several standards of accommodation are available.

4 Monarch Wildlife Cruises

Monarch Wildlife Cruises explore Otago Harbour all the way out past Taiaroa Head, observing the shags, petrels, shearwaters, albatross and other bird species that frequent the area. You may also see dolphins, seals and penguins. Trips begin from the city or from the jetty at Wellers Rock which is 45 minutes drive from Dunedin.

5 Sandfly Bay

From the carpark at the end of Seal Point Road a track leads down to some massive sand dunes which need to be crossed to reach Sandfly Bay. Don't worry, our pesky little flying friends are not the reason for the bay's name. That honour goes to the sand blown around by the strong winds that hit the ocean side of the peninsula. You may observe sea-lions, seals, penguins and other seabirds in the area, but please keep your distance. Allow 40 minutes to walk from the carpark to the far end of Sandfly Bay. Climbing back up the dune is a good struggle.

6 Sandymount Circuit – The Chasm and Lovers Leap

At the end of Sandymount Road a track leads around the summit of Sandymount, via the Chasm and Lovers Leap – two interesting natural features created from the eroding volcanic rock. From the carpark they can be reached in 20 minutes one way or 1 hour for the round trip. A side track leads down to Sandfly Bay.

7 Glenfalloch Woodland Garden and Café

This 'garden of national significance' is a wonderful blend of New Zealand and exotic flora – oak, walnut and birch trees, various natives, and even a 1000-year-old native matai tree. For more than 120 years this 12-ha garden has been carefully planned, nurtured and protected, and is open for public enjoyment. Located 15 minutes from the city along Portobello Road, the café is open for coffee or wine between 11 am and 3.30 pm during Summer.

8 1908 Restaurant

This is possibly the best restaurant on the peninsula, occupying an historic post office building in the small village of Portobello. Hearty main courses and delicious desserts are complemented by personal service.

The Catlins is the central part of what has become known as the Southern Scenic Route, an extensive stretch of countryside along the southern coastline between Dunedin and Invercargill. Its wild and scenic treasures remain relatively undiscovered – in fact the last section of SH 92 was not sealed until 2005.

Being less well known, this part of New Zealand may be low on your priority list – it shouldn't be. There are too many special features along this touring route to cover fully, so only some of the highlights are mentioned below. Grab a Southern Scenic Route brochure for extra details and spend a couple of days exploring. Accommodation options are increasing, but there are still few, so book ahead.

The Catlins area got its name from Captain Edward Cattlin, who bought land in this area from local Maori people in 1840. Unfortunately he died in Sydney in 1856 so never took possession of it. That didn't stop the authorities officially transferring the land into his name in 1873, a little too late for the captain.

❶ Waipapa Point

In 1881 this beautiful sandy beach witnessed the unfortunate drowning of 131 people when the *SS Tararua* hit a nearby reef. Drowning was known as the 'New Zealand death' during the 1800s, as unbridged rivers and uncharted coasts took a heavy toll. After the *Tararua* disaster a lighthouse was built as a memorial to the victims and to warn other ships.

❷ Slope Point

Marker posts lead the way across private farmland for 10 minutes to reach the southernmost tip of the South Island. Slope Point is 7 km further south than Bluff, and on a fine day you can see Stewart Island. Curiously-shaped trees demonstrate the power of the gale-force winds that regularly blow up from the direction of Antarctica.

❸ Curio Bay and Porpoise Bay

At low tide in Curio Bay you can explore a rocky shelf of fossilised trees from the Jurassic period 180 million years ago. The trees were similar to kauri, and the wood has been replaced entirely by silica, allowing them to resist the weathering effects of the ocean longer than the surrounding bedrock. The fossils are very interesting, but should not be taken as souvenirs.

During summer and autumn you may see Hector's dolphins cruising Porpoise Bay and surfing the waves. These dolphins are one of the smallest and rarest varieties in the world so please don't swim with them or feed them.

❹ McLean Falls

Rewcastle Road will take you to the McLean Falls Track, an easy 20–30 minute walk through forest to perhaps the best waterfall in the Catlins area.

THE CATLINS (SOUTHERN SCENIC ROUTE)

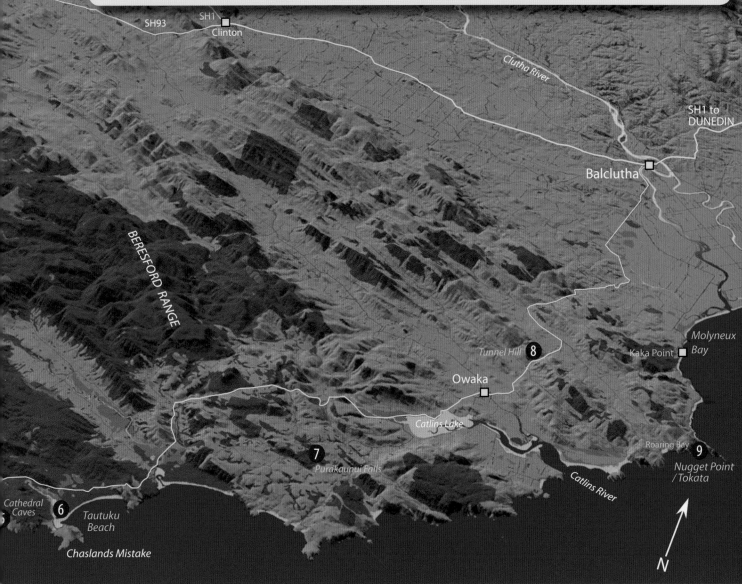

5 Cathedral Caves at Waipati Beach

The Cathedral Caves are accessed via private land, hence there is a small charge for parking and car security. After walking through native bush down a track to Waipati Beach turn left and walk along to these wonderful caves that rise around 30 metres above you. The caves are only accessible within 2 hours either side of low tide. Allow 1.5 hours for the return trip, take a torch and keep clear of any sea lions.

6 Tautuku Estuary Boardwalk

This estuary at the entrance of the Fleming River is frequented by the elusive fernbird. A track and boardwalk installed by the Forest and Bird Protection Society takes you right out to a platform in the middle of the estuary. From this platform you can see native forest on the far side of the river and hear the abundant birdlife – the morning chorus is the best time. It's a quiet, peaceful place. A little further east is Tautuku Beach, which can be reached via a track through virgin native forest.

7 Purakaunui Falls Scenic Reserve

An easy 10-minute walk through native forest will bring you to the Purakaunui Falls. The water falls 20 metres into a pool over three sequential cascades.

8 Tunnel Hill

This is a fun diversion right beside the Southern Scenic Route. An easy 10-minute walk leads you to a 250-metre-long, brick-lined tunnel completed in 1895 and once part of the Balclutha-Tahakopa branch railway line. Take a torch to walk through. Beyond the northern end of the tunnel is private farmland.

9 Nugget Point/Tokata

After driving 8 km off the main road you will arrive at Molyneux Bay and the small settlement of Kaka Point. Turn right to arrive at a small carpark at the start of a 5-minute walk to the lighthouse at Nugget Point. The sheer drop each side of this rocky outcrop will reveal baby seals playing in the rock pools 75 metres below you. There are extensive views along the coastline in both directions, so binoculars would be useful to spot sea-lions, penguins and various pelagic bird species. On the south side of the point, at Roaring Bay, a DOC hide is available for viewing the rare yellow-eyed penguins as they come and go.

STEWART ISLAND/RAKIURA

Mason Bay

Rakeahua

South West Ar

Big Glory Bay

Those lucky few who experience New Zealand's third main island, only 35 km from the South Island, will not be disappointed. Not until 2002 did the government recognise the natural values of the island by legislating to protect around 85% of it within Rakiura National Park.

This relatively isolated island is home to around 400 people, who live in the only town, Oban, in Halfmoon Bay on the eastern side of the island. Dominated by the wilderness behind it, abundant birdlife and lush vegetation make Oban a wonderful place to simply sit and watch. Walking opportunities are plentiful though: you can select from short walks, half-day walks and 3–12 day hiking tracks.

You can get to Stewart Island by fixed-wing aircraft (20 minutes), helicopter flights (12 minutes), or catamaran ferry trip (1 hour). Each service has scheduled trips, but the flight companies also provide private charters if you wish to enjoy an extended scenic flight over the island or land at a remote beach for a hiking trip.

① Oban Short Walks
Grab a very handy little map of the town to find the easy local walks, though some tracks have uphill sections – check with a local. The Fuchsia (15 minutes one way) and Raroa (25 minutes one way) tracks combined take you through native bush and down to Watercress Bay; or follow the Golden Bay-Deep Bay track for views of Paterson Inlet. Walk or take a taxi around the road past Lonnekers Beach to join the track to Ackers Point Lighthouse (45 minutes one way). Penguins and sooty shearwaters make their nests around the coast and point, so take care not to disturb them.

② Ulva Island
This small island in Paterson Inlet is an Open Island Sanctuary managed by DOC, with a well-maintained track network. Rats and other pests have been eliminated, allowing the vegetation and birdlife to thrive. A 10-minute water taxi ride will get you there for independent walks and picnics, but those interested in learning more about the history, flora and fauna should join one of the local guided trips.

③ Minibus Tour
For a scenic and insightful introduction to the top spots and history around the greater Oban area try a minibus tour. Tours can include Observation Point, Horseshoe Bay and Lee Bay, where the giant chain sculpture is located. Mountain bikes, motor scooters and rental cars are also available for hire.

④ Guided or Independent Kayaking
Kayaking the coastline of Stewart Island will provide a whole new range of nature experiences as you explore bays, beaches and bush-covered river channels, while watching the marine animals and birdlife. Several companies provide guided trips for all-comers, and will rent kayaks to experienced people.

⑤ Multi-Day Hiking Trips
To really escape humanity, fit people should grab all the right gear and head for the 36-km Rakiura Track, a Great Walk requiring 3 days. Very fit and experienced people who love mud can take on the formidable North West Circuit which has 125 km of track – allow 9–12 days for this. Other options are available such as walking between Freshwater Landing and Mason Bay.

⑥ Water Taxis
With many isolated beaches, hiking tracks and scenic spots spread around the coastline and inaccessible by road, water taxis are the most efficient and convenient way to reach them. Favourite destinations include Ulva Island, the Freshwater River (Paterson Inlet) for the track to Mason Bay, and historic Millars Beach.

⑦ Fishing, Hunting, Diving and Nature Cruises
Licensed launch operators can facilitate these activities in some fantastic spots around the coast. Scuba and fishing gear can be hired from the launch operators. Hunters need to apply in advance for a hunting permit.

RUGGEDY MOUNTAINS

RAKIURA NATIONAL PARK

Freshwater River

North Arm

Rakiura Track

5

Millars
Beach

Paterson Inlet

Port
William

Lee
Bay

Golden Bay

4

Oban

3

Horseshoe Bay

6

Ulva Island

Deep Bay

1

2

Halfmoon Bay

Ackers Point

7

The Neck

Bullers Point

N

ACKNOWLEDGEMENTS

Staff from i-Site visitor information centres, regional tourism organisations and Department of Conservation
offices have assisted with information in this book. For this support I am greatly appreciative.
Also, while I see myself as a professional inbound tour-guide, professional writer I was not.
Thanks are due to the team at Craig Potton Publishing: Tina Delceg who suggested
I write this book in the first place, Roger Smith for his map-making expertise,
Arnott Potter for editing expertise, Gwen Redshaw for the layout
and Robbie Burton and Phillippa Duffy for their encouragement.